MAP OF
PAKISTAN

50 0 50 100 150

SCALE IN MILES

80°   85°   35°   30°   25°   20°

C

H

I

N

A

OUNDARY UNDEFINED

N E P A L

SIKKIM

BHUTAN

ASSAM

BURMA

PAKISTAN

Rajshahi

DACCA

Khulna

TRIPURA

Chittagong

D I A

BAY OF BENGAL

80°   85°   90°

PAKISTAN
PERSPECTIVE

PAKISTAN
PERSPECTIVE

A collection of important articles
and excerpts from major addresses

by

Mohammad Ayub Khan
President of Pakistan

Printed in the United States of America
by the Embassy of Pakistan
Washington, D. C.

The world will find us frank and honest in our dealings with it. An undertaking, once given, shall be honored, whatever the cost. Pakistan expects the same from others.

Mohammad Ayub Khan

CONTENTS

"I BELIEVE . . ."   ix

I. PAKISTAN PERSPECTIVE
    Pakistan Perspective   3
    The Pakistan-American Alliance   17

II. AFRICA AND ASIA
    A Review   37
    Problems of Freedom   40

III. THE KASHMIR DISPUTE
    Kashmir Upheaval   47
    Kashmir and Peace   54
    Appeal to Reason   58
    Need for Realism   60
    Critical Juncture   63
    Fresh Approach   66

IV. INDIA'S MILITARY BUILD-UP
    Arming India   71
    Massive Build-Up   73
    A Period of Anxiety   75
    The Choice   77

V. ECONOMIC DEVELOPMENT
    Emerging Patterns   83
    Anatomy of Development   87
    Trade Versus Aid   89
    Economic Break-through   91
    Peace Through Prosperity   93
    Economic Liberalism   99
    Regional Cooperation   103

INDEX   107

"I BELIEVE . . ." *

I BELIEVE that Allah, in His infinite mercy, created Pakistan to give the Muslims of these regions a homeland in which to mould their lives in accordance with the fundamental principles and the spirit of Islam;

that Pakistan is destined to play a glorious role in the history of mankind and in particular in the advancement and progress of Muslims all over the world;

that the will of the people is supreme in all matters of the State;

that democracy provides the surest means of securing the fullest participation of the people in the affairs of their country;

that whatever the institutional form democracy may take in Pakistan, it must be based on pragmatism rather than dogmatism and must safeguard the basic right of the people to freedom of speech, freedom of association and freedom of assembly under the rule of law;

that the people of Pakistan must themselves determine the form of government which should be established consistent with the ideological basis of the country and the fundamental need for preserving the sovereignty, security and unity of the country;

that the people of Pakistan must move, as fast as possible, into the age of science and technology, while steadfastly preserving the basic tenets of their faith, in order to attain a higher standard of living;

that all class distinctions should disappear and Pakistanis should live and prosper as a model community symbolizing Islamic brotherhood and equality of man;

that there must be complete equality of opportunities available to all citizens of Pakistan;

that Pakistan should develop into a welfare state where basic necessities are available to all.

* Manifesto issued on the eve of the Presidential election in Pakistan, January 1965.

ix

I maintain that the reforms such as the land reforms, educational reforms, constitutional reforms and administrative reforms introduced during the last six years are aimed at freeing the society from the shackles of past domination, and elimination of class tensions and conflicts;

that further progress, in pursuit of the beliefs I have enunciated, would be possible only if we develop sufficient self-reliance to study our own problems and to solve them in our own way;

that only an enlightened approach based on practical realism rather than dominated by theorization, will help us to shed retrograde and antiquated traditionalism and usher in an era of true liberation: political, cultural, social, economic and intellectual;

that in all material and economic matters our attitude should not be doctrinaire but one dictated by the basic requirements of the situation;

that Pakistan's sovereignty and unity as a nation can be guaranteed only by a strong Center capable of providing full provincial autonomy without allowing centrifugal forces to re-assert themselves;

that in our dealings with other countries the determining factor must always be the interest of Pakistan and that we must always endeavor to enlarge the areas of understanding and friendship with other countries, particularly those who are our neighbors;

that we must work toward the establishment of world peace and human happiness and strive in all possible ways to save mankind from the horrors of war.

x

I undertake to maximize the utilization of national resources;

to provide for the widest possible and most equitable distribution of wealth;

to adopt all practical means to raise the income of the common man so as to reduce the disparity between the rich and the poor;

to ensure that the burden of taxation is distributed in a fair and equitable manner;

to eliminate cartels and monopolies;

to rationalize the land revenue system so as to give a fair deal especially to the small land-holder;

to adopt all practical measures to prevent the recurrence of floods in East Pakistan and to provide, as far as possible, adequate facilities for the rehabilitation of those affected by this menace;

to adopt all such measures as may be necessary to control water-logging and salinity in West Pakistan and to reclaim affected areas as far as possible;

to ensure the stability of the prices of goods used by the common man and to prevent inflation to the extent possible;

to take steps for the rehabilitation of homeless people and to provide better housing facilities;

to ensure that improvement in the standard of living of the people is not neutralized by unbalanced increase in population;

to associate local people in the administration of their affairs and to transfer gradually such functions as may be possible to the Basic Democracies;

to expand further the scope of rural works program in financial as well as functional terms;

to build up a strong rural community capable of looking after its own needs;

to provide greater educational facilities as envisaged in the Outline of the Third Five-Year Plan;

to work out a code of ethics for the press and to establish a voluntary machinery within the press itself to regulate effectively its conduct according to the code;

to take further measures to root out corruption in all branches of the Administration and to raise the standard of efficiency in the public services;

to take expeditious steps to achieve parity between the two wings of the country in the light of the constitutional provisions and to ensure that the pace of progress of the various regions of West Pakistan, as a single indivisible Unit, is increased further to bring about a balanced pattern of growth throughout the country;

to provide growing facilities for cultural integration and for the promotion of original and creative thinking;

to advance the ideology of Muslim nationalism which will enable Pakistan to serve as a strong base for collaboration with other Muslim countries of the world;

to support all liberal causes and to provide whatever assistance may be possible to such people or communities as may be in bondage or under the yoke of colonialism, imperialism or any other form of domination;

to continue to strive for the right of self-determination for the people of Jammu and Kashmir, and for its exercise in accordance with the UNCIP [United Nations Commission for India and Pakistan] resolutions and to provide all moral support to the freedom fighters of Kashmir;

to provide full protection and safeguards to minorities in Pakistan and to ensure for them equal opportunities, rights and privileges.

*I **urge** for Patience. Growth and development need time and not all the benefits can be secured by one generation. We have to work not only for ourselves but also for those who will follow us, and the thought that most of the benefits of our efforts may be reaped by the coming generations should be the mainstay of our effort;*

for Faith. We must have faith in ourselves and in our destiny, and whatever the community might embark upon should be a source of pride and satisfaction to all of us;

for Moderation. Reforms should be undertaken in a missionary and not in a vainglorious spirit. The objective should be to produce a better arrangement rather than to destroy an existing arrangement;

for National Outlook. We cannot afford to think in terms of provinces or regions. The economic advancement which we have already achieved has taken us to a stage where further progress will depend on our ability to evolve a national outlook, a national vision and to secure national unity;

for Hardwork. Empty slogans and fond hopes will get us nowhere. It is only through hard work undertaken in a selfless spirit and in the service of the community that we can achieve results.

It is in an endeavor to reach the objectives which I have outlined above that I am seeking re-election to the office of the President of Pakistan. My sole aim is to establish the sovereignty of the people and to work for the progress of Pakistan and the happiness and prosperity of the people of Pakistan.

Mohammad Ayub Khan

xiii

I.

Pakistan
Perspective

PAKISTAN PERSPECTIVE*

I AM not sure if the peculiar strains which confronted Pakistan immediately on its emergence as a free state are adequately understood. The first strain was ideological. It is a common fallacy to believe that the concept of Pakistan was formed in a poet's dream. The poet, Dr. Muhammad Iqbal, was no idle dreamer. Nor can countries like Pakistan (364,737 square miles; population 80,000,000) spring from the nebulous realm of poetry alone. Iqbal was in fact a philosopher of traditional as well as modern thought who had made a careful study of human affairs, both East and West, and focussed the light of his inquiry on the causes of economic and cultural subjugation to which the Muslims of India had been systematically subjected since their first abortive struggle for independence in 1857. It was in his presidential address to the annual session of All-India Muslim League in 1930 that he spelt out the broad outlines of a plan under which the Muslims of India were led to aspire to an independent state in which they would be free to follow their own way of life.

The All-India Muslim League based its Charter on this idea and, under the leadership of Quaid-i-Azam Mahomed Ali Jinnah, launched a struggle which culminated in the establishment of Pakistan in August 1947.

Iqbal's thesis that in their free state the Muslims were to practice their own way of life posed an ideological problem which was not easy to handle. On the one hand, there were many outside Pakistan who charged us with planning to establish an obdurate theocracy in the mediæval sense of the term. On the other, most of us within Pakistan itself were not quite clear how to go about welding our spiritual ideals into

* First appeared in *Foreign Affairs, July* 1960.

the business of statecraft. The result was a great deal of loose groping which infected our politics and our intellect alike.

Pakistan was thus involved in the paradox of almost losing its ideology in the very act of trying to fulfill it. This distraction was totally unwarranted, for Iqbal, one of the main creators of our ideology, had taken pains to define it in very clear terms:

> In Islam the spiritual and the temporal are not two distinct domains and the nature of an act, however, secular in its import, is determined by the attitude of mind with which the agent does it. It is the invisible mental background of the act which ultimately determines its character. An act is temporal or profane if it is done in a spirit of detachment from the infinite complexity of life behind it. It is spiritual if it is inspired by that complexity. In Islam it is the same reality which appears as Church looked at from one point of view and State from another.

According to this concept, the State owes a singular and specific duty to its people. "The essence of Tauhid (Unity of God) as a working idea is equality, solidity and freedom," according to Iqbal. "The State from the Islamic standpoint is an endeavor to transform these ideals into space-time forces, an aspiration to realize them in a definite human organization."

It is this sort of human organization which Pakistan aspires to become and one of my endeavors is to clear at least a part of the way by liberating the basic concept of our ideology from the dust of vagueness and ambiguities it has accumulated over the years.

The second strain which befell Pakistan immediately on its emergence was economic. Besides more than 9,000,000 refugees who poured over the border in a state of appalling terror and distress, food fell desperately short owing to hundreds of thousands of acres of land going out of use every year on account of salinity and water-logging, a menace

which still continues unabated. As much as 10,000,000 acres
of good fertile land have already fallen out of cultivation on
this account. Moreover, successive governments were unable
to control the situation adequately, and large-scale organized
smuggling, currency rackets, black-marketing and increasingly
plastic standards of honesty and efficiency brought the affairs
of the country to the verge of total ruin.

The third strain—which is a continuous one—is geographical. Divided into two wings (West Pakistan: 310,236 square
miles, population 38,779,000; East Pakistan: 54,501 square
miles, population 42,063,000), there are over 1,000 miles of
India in-between without any assured means of land communications. Air travel is heavily subsidized but still too
expensive for most people. The sea link involves a journey of
about seven days. There is diversity of languages, scripts and
social customs. By the very nature of things, these factors
are centrifugal and call for a new and bold experiment with
political and administrative science to weave unity out of
diversity. The situation is often difficult but not baffling, for
a common ideology provides a positive base for cohesion.
The firmness of this base is strong or weak accordingly as
that ideology is understood and practiced rightly or wrongly.

Finally, there is the emotional factor. Till the advent of
Pakistan, none of us was in fact a Pakistani, for the simple
reason that there was no territorial entity bearing that name.
Actually, the boundaries of Pakistan were still being drawn
and re-drawn secretly in the Viceregal Lodge at New Delhi
when independence was proclaimed. Never had the destiny
of so many millions depended so helplessly on the arbitrary
strokes of one man's pencil. It was because Mr. Radcliffe
happened to make a small dent on the wrong side of the line
that over 4,000,000 inhabitants of Jammu and Kashmir have
been locked in a life-and-death struggle for self-determination
for 13 long and dreadful years.

So, prior to 1947, our nationalism was based more on an idea than on any territorial definition. Till then, ideologically we were Muslims; territorially we happened to be Indians; and parochially we were a conglomeration of at least eleven smaller, provincial loyalties. But when suddenly Pakistan emerged as a reality, we who had got together from every nook and corner of the vast sub-continent were faced with the task of transforming all our traditional, territorial and parochial loyalties into one great loyalty for the new state of Pakistan. This process of metamorphism was naturally attended by difficult psychological and emotional strains which we have borne in full measure—and are still bearing.

Under normal circumstances, it would have required most extraordinary efforts by the best of governments to cope with the problems which have been confronting us. But unfortunately neither have our circumstances been normal, nor did we have good strong governments; and they did not make even ordinary efforts to resolve the problems in front of them.

The founder of Pakistan, Quaid-i-Azam Mahomed Ali Jinnah, was already a sick man on the eve of his triumph. He died within about a year. His Prime Minister, Liaquat Ali Khan, who had been closest to him during the struggle for independence, fell to an assassin's bullet in 1951. This created a vacuum in top leadership; and in smaller hands party politics became a mad scramble for power. Government after government rose and fell and within a period of five years six Prime Ministers presided over precariously balanced cabinets. The real and pressing problems of the country were ignored in this hide and seek for power.

It is now the fashion to blame the politicians outright for this mess. Yes, they were guilty of many misdeeds of omission and commission; but there is one fundamental point in which, I have a feeling, they were rather sinned against than sinning. That is, they were given a system of government totally unsuited to the temper and climate of the country.

The British parliamentary system which we inherited and later adopted in the Constitution of 1956 is largely an unwritten law and takes for granted too many prerequisites which do not really exist in a country like Pakistan. Our rate of literacy is appallingly low. Our means of communication are poor, even primitive. The rural population which constitutes over 80 per cent of the total is hardly touched by the world outside the villages.

Just before independence, when Mr. Jinnah was anxious to put more and more of his party men in the Central and Provincial Assemblies of India to carry on the struggle for the idea of Pakistan, he issued an appeal: "Vote for a Muslim Leaguer even if it be a lamp-post." People complied cheerfully; some even literally! When independence came, the gentlemen thus elected found themselves in a position of vantage to assume power in the new state of Pakistan, and the political system in their hands enabled them to keep delaying the making of a constitution for about eight years. The outgoing Parliament of Pakistan had 80 seats, each member presuming to represent about a million of his countrymen for almost an indefinite period. Even under the Constitution of 1956, a member of the Provincial Assembly was required to be elected by more than 100,000 voters. Now this is the type of electoral college which just cannot work in Pakistan— or for that matter in any country where conditions like those of Pakistan obtain, as they do in many newly independent countries of Asia and Africa. An average villager with little or no education has no means of gaining any personal knowledge about a candidate who is mixed up in a population of 100,000 or more, spread over a large area without any advanced means of communication and contact. Votes cast under these circumstances cannot but be vague, wanton and responsive to fear, coercion, temptation and other modes of misguidance. This is exactly what had been happening in Pakistan. Whenever elections were held, they could be easily manipulated to return candidates with power to influence, money to bribe and nuisance value to coerce. Conditions such as these reduce the practice of democracy to a farce.

But this does not dismay us. Nor should it be taken to imply that we can do—or wish to do—without democracy. The revolution of October 7, 1958, was not aimed against the institution of democracy as such. No, it was only against the manner in which its institutions were being worked. There are two main reasons why we in Pakistan cannot but adhere to a democratic pattern of life and government. In the first place, as Muslims, we are brought up on two basic ingredients of democracy, namely, equality and fraternity. Anything to the contrary would be the negation of our spiritual faith and practice. And, secondly, we have to fight a long and arduous battle for progress and development in which every man, woman and child of Pakistan must participate to the fullest possible extent. Democracy provides the only healthy and dignified way for arousing the willing cooperation of people and harnessing it to a sustained national endeavor.

We must, therefore, have democracy. The question then is: What type of democracy? The answer need not be sought in the theories and practices of other people alone. On the contrary, it must be found from within the book of Pakistan itself.

To my mind, there are four prerequisites for the success of any democratic system in a country like Pakistan:

1. It should be simple to understand, easy to work and cheap to sustain.

2. It should put to the voter only such questions as he can answer in the light of his own personal knowledge and understanding without external prompting.

3. It should ensure the effective participation of all citizens

in the affairs of the country up to the level of their mental horizon and intellectual calibre.

4. It should be able to produce reasonably strong and stable governments.

The scheme of "basic democracies" which has been launched in Pakistan is designed to meet most of these fundamental prerequisites. Under this scheme, the two wings of the country have each been divided into 40,000 constituencies with an average population of about 1,000. Every constituency elects one representative by universal franchise. In such a small and well-defined field of choice, voters of the meanest intelligence cannot go far wrong in putting their finger on the right type of candidate.

Ten such constituencies form a Union Council in the rural areas, and this elects its own chairman from amongst the elected members. Provision has also been made for nominated members to ensure, where necessary, the representation of special interests, like women, minorities, etc. In towns and larger municipalities organization follows a similar pattern.

The elected chairmen of Union Councils and Town Committees represent their areas on the next tier of administration, namely, the Thana Council, which covers the entire area under the jurisdiction of a Police Station. From this stage, this system of associating the chosen representatives of the people with local administration travels upwards covering all intermediary tiers, like tehsils, districts and divisions, up to the provincial level. This is designed to ensure a full sense of cooperation between the official and elected agencies at all stages of public administration.

The first elections to basic democracies were held last December and I feel the results were quite heartening. The average percentage of votes cast was 67 per cent by men and

42 per cent by women. Those elected included 14 per cent university graduates, 78 per cent literate and 8 per cent illiterate members. They came from the real hard core of the country, the majority of them being middle-class and lower middle-class agriculturists, lawyers, medical practitioners, business-men, retired government servants, workers and artisans.

One great lesson which these elections brought out was that, for the first time in Pakistan, it seemed possible for an average citizen to seek election purely on his or her personal merit without the help of any financial, social or political backing. Also for the first time, the elected candidate finds himself in a position to participate effectively and directly in the affairs of the country as they exist immediately around him.

The Union Councils and Town Committees have been given a wide charter of duties and responsibilities ranging from local self-government to national reconstruction and development. Besides this, I am looking to this gigantic instrument of mass representation to achieve three other pressing objectives. First, to help throw up a fresh supply of local and national leaders. Second, to serve as a two-way traffic post between the government and the basic core of the people and to bridge the gulf which under the best of systems is bound to exist between them in countries where education is limited, distances are large and modern facilities for reaching the masses are not universal. And, third, I would personally like this body of 80,000 elected representatives to serve as the electoral college for the Parliament and, possibly, for the President. This is only my personal view, for I do not wish to pre-judge the recommendations of the Constitution Commission which is at the moment seized of this and other allied problems.

The Constitution Commission of Pakistan, consisting of

eminent judges, lawyers and other interests, was set up in
February this year and has been entrusted with the following
terms of reference:

> To examine the progressive failure of the parliamentary
> government in Pakistan leading to the abrogation of the
> Constitution of 1956 and to determine the causes and the
> nature of the failure;

> To consider how best the said or like causes may be
> identified and their recurrence prevented;

> And, having further taken account of the genius of the
> people, the general standard of education and of political
> judgment in the country, the present state of a sense of
> nationhood, the prime need for sustained development, and
> the effect of the constitutional and administrative changes
> brought into being in recent months, to submit constitutional
> proposals in the form of a report advising how best the
> following ends may be secured: a democracy adaptable to
> changing circumstances and based on the Islamic princi-
> ples of justice, equality and tolerance; the consolidation of
> national unity; and a firm and stable system of government.

I trust that toward the end of this year we shall be in a
position to determine the broad shape of our future constitutional pattern. I would like to move as fast as possible, but
there are many in our country who look askance at this haste.
Some of them fear that politicians may return and mess things
up once again. Others suspect that reforms and innovations
introduced under the Martial Law may backslide and that
the development program may slow down with the return of
normal conditions.

These misgivings are understandable, but I do not feel
they are well-founded. The former politicians are no problem
to us now or in the near future. We have taken good care to
spare them the usual tragic fate of those overtaken by revolu-
tionary upheavals. On the contrary, we are content to treat
them as a big joke, just as they turned a perfectly sound

country into the laughing-stock of the whole world. When they are confronted with skeletons collected from their cupboards, most of them wisely prefer to retire from public life for five to six years rather than face the risk of open trial. This saves a lot of dirty linen from being washed publicly, and decent folk prefer this quiet exit of errant politicians.

As regards the suspicion that the return of constitutional rule might undo or retard the progress of reforms launched under the Martial Law, this again is an unreal fear. These reforms were long overdue and have been fully and unequivocally acclaimed by the people. No future government dare retard or obstruct them. The only prerequisite is that the government should be strong enough to resist the pressure of vested interests which have been hit hard by some of the reforms. This, I am positive, the new Constitution must ensure.

Moreover, when circumstances such as our revolution concentrate power in the hands of one person, it is his bounden duty to pass that power on to a more broadly based system without avoidable delay. Individuals are fallible; but institutions stay. That is why I am in such a hurry to ensure the induction of a suitable constitutional system without any loss of time.

While the Constitution is still in the making, there is time to complete the reforms already in hand or give a start to those which are still under contemplation. The meaning of all this activity is to prepare the ground for the growth of a happy and healthy life which, after all, is the end-product of all human endeavor.

An archaic type of feudalism which existed in Pakistan—particularly West Pakistan—had vested the entire political, economic and social might of the country in a limited group of families. It was impossible to make any advance in any direction without first breaking this monopoly of power.

Therefore, land reform was one of the first measures to be taken by the new regime. This was a major operation but it was performed peacefully and scientifically and was attended by no manner of tyranny or injustice. This is a far-reaching socio-economic change and its full impact will be felt only with the passage of time.

Other fields in which reforms have been undertaken include education, public health, fiscal systems, law courts, civil administration and the rehabilitation of refugees. The object is to get us to the starting point of development, whence we may be better able to grapple with some of the most pressing and immediate of our problems. These are: fighting the grave menace to the land of salinity and water-logging; curbing the excessive rate of growth of population; and launching the next Five Year Plan for national development, estimated to cost over 19,000,000,000 rupees (about $4,000,000,000). According to experts, these figures are not astronomical but only reasonable.

The next 15 to 20 years are going to be most crucial for Pakistan. Either we "make the grade" in this period or we do not. If we fail to make the grade, we are bound to be submerged under the tidal wave of Communism which is constantly lashing its fury all around us. Since we do not seek this fate we must move forward, and do so quickly. It is here that our eyes turn towards our friends and allies. They have already given us magnanimous aid, for which we are most grateful. But there are reasons of history which entitle us to claim still more.

During the last 200 years or so the area which is now Pakistan was subjected to foreign rule. This stunted our growth immeasurably and all this long period of time was lost to us for preparing ourselves to move with the modern scientific times. We have now to catch up with the fast-moving world—

and this will require extraordinary endeavor as well as expenditure.

It was during the period of imperial rule that the British industrial development started and gained momentum with resources which to a large extent were taken from the colonial areas. The British industrial development in a way gave a fillip to the American industrial development. It is common knowledge that up to the Second World War, Britain had enormous investments in both the Americas. Most of the progress in the Commonwealth countries and Dominions was also stimulated by the British industrial development. So far as the area now forming Pakistan is concerned, its manpower was generally employed to man the British Armies to maintain and protect the Empire. For this reason, this part of the Indo-Pakistan sub-continent was purposely kept industrially backward so that the populace would not be diverted into other channels of employment.

Moreover, in the context of present-day world politics Pakistan has openly and unequivocally cast its lot with the West, and unlike several other countries around us, we have shut ourselves off almost completely from the possibility of any major assistance from the Communist bloc. We do not believe in hunting with the hound and running with the hare. We wish to follow, and are following, a clear and unambiguous path.

All these factors lead to one conclusion: that the English-speaking world ought to feel a special responsibility to assist Pakistan in attaining a reasonable posture of advancement. It is not just a claim. It is in fact the dictate of history.

Before I conclude, I would like to add a few words about our relations with our neighbors. I am quite clear in my mind that in order to be able to make some progress at home, we must have a long spell of undisturbed peace around us. But unfortunately our relations with India and Afghanistan have not been good. We have approached them and made every effort, without success, to get a settlement on mutually honorable and reasonable terms.

As regards Afghanistan, I really do not understand why there should be any trouble between us at all. The rulers of Afghanistan have woven so many vague and imaginary webs of grievances and demands that they now fancy they are inextricably caught in them. Somehow they suspect us and fear that a strong Pakistan would be a danger to Afghanistan. As a matter of fact, the truth is just the other way round. But we have not succeeded in bringing home this truth to the Afghan rulers. Let us hope they will see the light before it is too dark.

We have made some little progress with India in certain fields but we are stuck over the problem of Kashmir. There is some reluctance on the part of Indian leadership to move forward and discuss this problem in a spirit of realism and justice. They do not seem to realize that a running sore like this between two neighbors is a dangerous thing.

I think there is room and need for India and Pakistan to live as friends. If we cannot live as good friends, at least we should have a decent, human, neighborly relationship with each other. This is what we, on our part, are trying to develop. But this has so far remained a largely unilateral endeavor. We have had very little response from the other side. This does not dismay me. I still hope that one day realism will dawn in India too.

As a student of war and strategy, I can see quite clearly the inexorable push of the north in the direction of the warm waters of the Indian Ocean. This push is bound to increase if India and Pakistan go on squabbling with each other. If, on the other hand, we resolve our problems and disengage our armed forces from facing inwards as they do today, and face them outwards, I feel we shall have a good chance of preventing a recurrence of the history of the past, which was that whenever this sub-continent was divided—and often it was divided—someone or other invited an outsider to step in.

THE PAKISTAN-AMERICAN ALLIANCE*

I T is nearly ten years since Pakistan became an ally of the West. In May 1954, Pakistan signed the Mutual Defense Assistance Agreement with the United States. Later in that year it became a member of SEATO along with the United States, Britain, France, Thailand, the Philippines, Australia and New Zealand. A year later, it joined the Baghdad Pact, another mutual defense organization, with Britain, Turkey, Iran and Iraq. The United States has not joined this organization, but has remained closely associated with it since its inception. In 1958, when Iraq left this pact, it was renamed CENTO (Central Treaty Organization): it continued to comprise Turkey, Iran and Pakistan as its regional members. Early in 1959, Pakistan signed (as did Turkey and Iran) a bilateral Agreement of Cooperation with the United States, which was designed further to reinforce the defensive purposes of CENTO.

Thus Pakistan is associated with the United States through not one, but four mutual security arrangements. In this sense, it has been sometimes termed "America's most allied ally in Asia." It is the only Asian country which is a member both of SEATO and CENTO.

The strategic location of Pakistan is of some significance in this connection. West Pakistan borders on the Middle East, is close to Soviet Russia's southern frontier and shares a common border with China. It stands across the great mountain passes through which all land invasions of the Indo-Pakistan sub-continent have taken place in recorded history. East Pakistan, on the other hand, borders on Burma. Thus West Pakistan and East Pakistan flank India on her northwest and on her northeast. So situated, Pakistan virtually constitutes a defensive shield for India. It constitutes also the gateway to South Asia.

* First appeared in *Foreign Affairs*, January 1964

It should therefore be in the interest of world peace, particularly of India's security, that Pakistan remain strong and stable.

Nevertheless, Pakistan came in for bitter criticism from India when she joined these purely defensive alliances. India charged that by so doing "Pakistan had brought the cold war to the sub-continent." The real purpose of this Indian outcry became clearer, however, as time advanced, and more particularly when in 1959 Pakistan signed the bilateral Agreement of Cooperation. According to this agreement, the United States would under certain circumstances assist Pakistan if she became the victim of aggression. India demanded and, according to Mr. Nehru, received a "specific assurance" from Washington that this pact "could not be used against India."[1] Shorn of sophistry, this demand amounted to seeking an assurance that if India should commit aggression against Pakistan or threatened Pakistan's security, the United States would not come to the assistance of Pakistan under this pact. There could not be a more illuminating commentary on India's historic attitude toward Pakistan.

This attitude also explains why India has throughout opposed the grant of military aid to Pakistan. It is not that she feared that Pakistan—a fifth her size and with armed forces a quarter the size of hers—would, through the kind of military aid program the United States contemplated, become a serious military threat to India. In actual fact the military aid to Pakistan was designed to give her merely a deterrent force. Even with the aid, the armed forces of Pakistan were not to be more than one-third of India's strength before her border clashes with China. Therefore, Pakistan could not possibly pose any threat to India.

The real reason behind India's opposition to Pakistan's receiving military aid was a combination of several factors, including the bitter opposition of the Hindu community to the

[1] Speaking in the Indian Parliament, March 14, 1959.

very creation of Pakistan, India's refusal to honor her solemn
pledges in respect of Jammu and Kashmir, and India's desire
to dominate what she considers to be her own sphere of
influence in Asia.

I have spoken of India's hostility to Pakistan's alliance with
the United States. She resorted also to direct pressure to prevent Pakistan from joining it. In August 1953, after bilateral
negotiations lasting over some months, Mr. Nehru and Mr.
Mohammad Ali, Pakistan's Prime Minister at that time, issued
a joint communique on Kashmir. In it, they agreed, *inter alia,*
that: "It was their firm opinion that this [Kashmir dispute]
should be settled in accordance with the wishes of the people
of that State. . . . The most feasible way of ascertaining the
wishes of the people was by fair and impartial plebiscite."
Further, "it was decided that the Plebiscite Administrator
should be appointed by the end of April 1954. . . . He will
then make such proposals as he thinks proper for preparations
to be made for the holding of a fair and impartial plebiscite in
the entire State and take such other steps as may be considered
necessary therefor."

Shortly thereafter, Mr. Nehru got wind of the fact that Pakistan was likely to enter into an alliance with the United States
and receive military aid from that country. In a protracted
correspondence with Mr. Mohammad Ali, he protested strongly and indicated that if Pakistan went ahead with that project,
their agreement on Kashmir would lapse.[2] Mr. Mohammad
Ali replied that he did not see why any military assistance that
Pakistan might receive from the United States for purely defensive purposes should make it less imperative for them to

[2] "We, in India, have endeavored to follow a foreign policy which we feel
is not only in the interests of world peace but is particularly indicated for
the countries of Asia. That policy is an independent one and of non-alignment with any power bloc. It is clear that the policy which Pakistan intends
to pursue is different. . . . It means that Pakistan is tied up in a military
sense with the U.S.A. and is aligned to that particular group of
powers. . . . This produces a qualitative change in the existing situation
and, therefore, it affects Indo-Pakistan relations, and, more especially,
the Kashmir problem." (Mr. Nehru's letter of December 21, 1953, to the
Pakistan Prime Minister.)

improve India-Pakistan relations by settling the Kashmir dispute. In particular, he did not see why, if Pakistan joined an alliance with the United States, this would disqualify the people of Kashmir from exercising their right—which the United Nations, India and Pakistan had acknowledged—to a free vote to decide whether their state should accede to India or Pakistan.

In December of that year—although Pakistan had not by then either entered into any pact with the United States or received any military assistance—Mr. Nehru indicated that he could not go forward with the agreements set out in the joint communique on Kashmir, because "the whole context in which these agreements were made will change if military aid comes [to Pakistan] from America."[3] Obviously Pakistan could not allow Mr. Nehru to dictate her foreign policy. In May 1954, Pakistan went ahead with the signing of the Mutual Defense Assistance Agreement with the United States. From that point on, the fact that the Indian Prime Minister would repudiate the joint communique on Kashmir became a foregone conclusion. Pakistan's efforts to save it eventually collapsed when the Prime Ministers met for the last time in May 1955.

In that same year the alliance with the United States came under heavier pressure. The Soviet Union reacted when, in 1955, Pakistan joined the Baghdad Pact (now called CENTO). Up to that time, the Soviet Union had maintained a neutral stand on the Kashmir dispute. Its representatives had abstained from voting whenever this issue came up in the Security Council. The Soviet Union charged that by joining the Baghdad Pact, Pakistan had become a member of "an aggressive Western alliance," and she responded by radically altering her stand on Kashmir. Thenceforth, the Soviet Union began to subscribe to India's claim that no plebiscite was possible or necessary in Kashmir and that

[3] Statement in the Indian Parliament, December 23, 1953.

Kashmir was an "integral part" of India. In pursuance of this new stand, the Soviet Union has, since then, vetoed every resolution of the Security Council on Kashmir to which India has objected—regardless of its merits. For some time, the Soviet Union's stand was that the Kashmir dispute was being exploited by the Western powers for their own ends and that she would prefer to see it decided through direct negotiations between India and Pakistan, without the intervention of those powers. In 1962, the Soviet Union went further. Obviously at the instance of India, she even vetoed the Security Council resolution of June 22, 1962, which, in essence, merely called upon India and Pakistan to settle this dispute through bilateral negotiations.

In contrast, over the last decade, the policies of the United States have undergone a change which has operated progressively to the disadvantage of her ally, Pakistan, vis-a-vis neutral India.

When we first joined the alliance with the United States, neutralism—"non-alignment" as India prefers to call it—was suspect in American eyes. It was in fact regarded as "immoral." It was another name for "playing both sides of the street." Over the years, it has come to assume a mantle of respectability in American eyes. Indeed, some four years ago it gradually began to occupy, in American estimation, a privileged position. The favor of neutral countries began to be actively sought, in some cases in competition against the Soviet Union. In particular, influential American circles began to advocate "massive aid" to India.

At the same time, there grew a feeling among the allies of the United States—not in Pakistan only—that, in a variety of ways, they were being increasingly taken for granted. Gradually, as a result of this change in American thinking, neutral India became the largest recipient by far of American economic aid, while she continued freely to castigate the United States in the United Nations and outside whenever opportunity offered. Pakistan watched this transformation in American foreign policy with increasing perplexity and dismay.

India regards herself as a big power in Asia. Her eventual aim has been, and still is, to have her sphere of influence in Southeast Asia. The Indian leaders have often stated that their true border extends from the Hindu Kush mountains to the Mekong River, that is to say, wherever the influence of Hinduism has existed in the past. Their earlier friendly overtures to China were based on the hope that there would be an understanding between them and China over their respective spheres of influence in Asia, and that China would recognize and endorse India's claim. They moreover felt that as long as the American influence existed in Asia, the achievement of any such objective would not be possible. That was the reason why India, although accepting aid from the United States, made strenuous efforts to oppose the United States on every major issue in the world forum and elsewhere in order to belittle her prestige and influence. If America lost face before the whole world it did not matter so long as her influence was reduced, if not eliminated altogether, in Asia.

It follows that as soon as India arrives at some sort of settlement with China, she will revert to the traditional policy of eliminating United States influence from Asia. It is for this reason that India's facade of neutrality is still maintained in spite of massive arms aid from the West and close collaboration in the military field. She has retained sufficient flexibility and political freedom to revert to her traditional anti-American policy as soon as circumstances permit. The receipt of arms and economic aid now is not going to make any more difference than the previous supply of military and economic aid made in India's open hostility to the United States.

In the past, if the United States gave economic aid to India we were not against it as such. We were concerned rather over its massiveness and scale. It enabled India to divert her own resources very substantially to the strengthening of her armed forces; she was, in effect, receiving indirect military aid. Our concern arose from the fact that the Indian military build-up was aimed solely against Pakistan. The pronouncements of Indian leaders and the continued massing of India's army on Pakistan's borders clearly suggested this.

Until the fall of 1962, however, the policy of the United States continued to distinguish somewhat between a "non-aligned" India and the American ally, Pakistan. Although under a Mutual Defense Assistance Agreement signed in 1951 (reaffirmed in 1958), India also was receiving certain military aid from the United States—without accepting any of the obligations that devolve on an ally—American policy continued generally to maintain, in the matter of *direct* military aid, a substantial difference between an ally and a neutral. An ally was qualified to receive military assistance on a scale that the United States considered justified in the light of that country's obligations under the alliance; a neutral, by and large, was not entitled to receive military aid on any commensurate scale. However, this remaining distinction between Pakistan and "non-aligned" India also disappeared last fall when the border disputes between India and China flared up into an armed clash.

Despite the fact that over the decade the distinction in American eyes between an ally and a neutral had become increasingly blurred to a vanishing point, Pakistan continued steadily to stand by the alliance. Our view has been that, so long as we are in this alliance, we must continue honorably to discharge so far as we can whatever obligations devolve on us as a member.

In the fall of 1962, however, Pakistan received a new cause for disillusionment with American foreign policy. Following the India-China border clash, the United States proceeded to rush arms to India on a scale which to us seemed totally unjustified by the requirements of the situation. Since then, arms aid has been flowing into India continuously on a very substantial scale, not only from the United States but also in almost equal measure from Britain and, to a small extent, from some other members of the Commonwealth. We are profoundly concerned over this new development. We consider that this continued arming of India, in which the Soviet Union has also, for reasons of her own, joined, poses a serious threat to Pakistan's security.

It is possible that some of our friends abroad are perplexed by this reaction. They may ask: Is not the military assistance given to India by Pakistan's allies meant exclusively for fighting Communist China? Has not India pledged that she will not use these arms against Pakistan? Have not the United States and Great Britain also given assurances that if India employed these weapons in an aggression against Pakistan, they would act to thwart the aggression? Are not these assurances, they may ask, sufficient to protect Pakistan against the possible misuse of Western arms against her? Why then, they may inquire, are the Pakistanis alarmed?

Before I proceed to answer this question, let me briefly recapitulate the facts leading up to the current Western policy of arming India in a major war.

On October 20, 1962, fighting flared up between China and India at a number of points along their disputed border, in Ladakh (Kashmir) and in the Northeast Frontier Agency (NEFA) area lying east of the state of Bhutan. A week earlier, Mr. Nehru announced that he had ordered the troops to throw the Chinese "out of our territory" in the NEFA area, and then left for Ceylon on a state visit.[4] There is some independent evidence also to the effect that the Indians opened the first attack. Why Mr. Nehru chose that particular time to make that announcement has been the subject of considerable conjecture. What prompted him to do so is, at any rate at this point, immaterial. What happened subsequently is, however, fairly generally known. During two brief bouts of fighting— the first in October and the second in November—the Indian

4 *Times of India,* October 13, 1962.

army met with serious reverses. By November 20, the Indians had surrendered another 2,000 square miles of disputed territory in Ladakh, thus putting the Chinese in control of almost the entire 15,000 square miles of territory which they claim in that part of Kashmir. In the NEFA area, the rout of the Indian forces assumed even more serious proportions. By November 20, not only the entire disputed NEFA territory but even Assam lay at the mercy of the rapidly advancing Chinese forces. Then, suddenly, on November 21, the Chinese declared a cease-fire and offered unilaterally to withdraw to points behind the MacMahon Line from the entire territory they had overrun. This undertaking they subsequently fully carried out, offering at the same time to negotiate their border differences with India peacefully. Since then, there has been no significant military incident on any part of the entire disputed border.

It was after the first India-China clash in October that the United States Government decided to rush military equipment to India. The British and to a minor extent some other countries also joined in what was called emergency assistance to India.

At Nassau on December 29, long after the cease-fire on the India-China border, the United States and Britain decided to continue to supply India on an emergency basis with up to $120,000,000 worth of military aid. The program included a variety of military equipment, but its central feature was the arming of six Indian divisions for mountain warfare. Arising also from the Nassau decision, a United States-British-Canadian Air Mission visited India to examine into what would be India's air needs should China attack again. And another U.S. Mission went out to India to study the question of how to expand India's arms production capacity.

Subsequently, on June 30, at Birch Grove, the United States and Britian decided on a further substantial program of military aid to India, over and above that agreed to at Nassau. Apart from additional arms, this program provides

for extensive radar, communications, air transport and train-
ing facilities as well as for American and British assistance to
expand greatly India's own armament production. India has
also been assured that there is no need for her to enter an
alliance with the West in order to continue to qualify for
military assistance against China. Indeed, she has been given
to understand that it is in the Western interest that she should
continue to remain "non-aligned" and receive military aid
from the Soviet Union as well. Taking advantage of this favorable Western response, India has decided to raise her standing
army from 11 to 22 divisions as rapidly as possible and to
expand substantially her air force and navy as well—all
ostensibly for use against China.

Let us first examine briefly whether the arming of India on
this extensive scale is necessary or justified. It may be recalled
that the American-British military aid program to India was
originally put in motion at a time when the West feared that
the India-China conflict might escalate into a major war. From
the very outset it has been our view that the fighting in 1962
was only in the nature of a border conflict. On November 5,
after the first India-China clash, I made a statement to that
effect, and expressed concern over the Western decision to
rush military aid to India on a scale based apparently on an
assumption that India was faced with a major war with China.
There was no valid basis for this assumption. It made no sense
militarily, I said, that China should have decided to launch
an invasion of India over the Himalayas in the depth of winter.
Under the circumstances it seemed logical to conclude that the
Chinese objectives were limited.

This, I consider, has been borne out by subsequent events.
The unilateral declaration of a cease-fire by the Chinese forces
at a time when not only the disputed territory but the whole
of northeastern India, including Assam, lay within their easy
grasp, their withdrawal from the entire NEFA territory which
they had overrun, and their offer to settle the dispute peace-

fully—none of this supports the thesis that the Chinese had planned to embark on a major attack on India. Since then, the Chinese military threat to India has, it is now generally recognized, receded. The Chinese have demonstrated their willingness to settle the dispute peacefully. The Indians, on their part, are anxious to avoid any further fighting with China and have been working steadily for a peaceful settlement. Yet India continues to demand—and receive—military assistance from the United States and Great Britain on a large scale and has embarked upon a massive increase and re-equipment of her land, air and naval forces. Considering the terms on which neutralist India is receiving this assistance—terms which amount virtually to a gift—the inducement to do so must be very strong.

India currently presents three faces to the world: one to the West, simulating a resolve to fight China in order to secure the maximum of Western arms assistance; a second to Russia, stressing her resolve nevertheless to remain "non-aligned"; and a third to China, seeking a peaceful settlement of the dispute by secret peace overtures through neutral emissaries.

The hope is held in certain quarters in the United States and Britain that the military assistance given or proposed would enable India to fight the Communist threat in South Asia. Some people in those countries fondly imagine that a "newly awakened" India would act as a rallying point for South Asian nations against Communist expansionism. In actual fact, India has no such intention.

Mr. Nehru himself has been at pains to explain that the India-China conflict has nothing to do with Communism but is the result of Chinese "imperialist expansionism."[5]

Last April a well-informed Indian journalist threw interesting light on the objectives of New Delhi's policy toward China. He had, among other things, this to say:

> Some of the truths of Mr. Nehru's earlier utterances need

[5] Philip Potter, in the *Baltimore Sun*, November 10, 1962.

28

Pakistan Perspective

to be repeated. One of these is that China, Communist or oherwise, aggressive or peaceful, is a neighbor with which somehow India must learn to live. It is a geographical truth that cannot be wished away. . . .

Visions of a devious and infinitely cunning Chinese plot to dominate India or Asia, thrilling theories of an Indian "way of life" threatened by an aggressive ideology from the north, interesting academic parallels between the Indian and Chinese race for economic development—all this sounds plausible but is liable to turn into so much fluff when thoroughly examined.

New Delhi's policy is, very rightly, to work for an understanding with a powerful neighbor. If this is not possible soon, as it probably is not, the alternative is patience, vigilance, adaptability and calm determination. It is most certainly not to set an ideological example for other Asian States to follow or to lead them in any kind of crusade or to interpret the Chinese aggression in the "perspective" most palatable to the United States.[6]

It is our belief that the Sino-Indian dispute can and will be resolved peacefully. In our view, therefore, the continuance of military aid to India is unjustified. Furthermore, it poses a grave threat to Pakistan's security. We apprehend that after India has settled her dispute with China, she will revert to her traditional policy of intimidation of Pakistan. And she may even turn her newly acquired might against Pakistan when a suitable opportunity occurs, particularly at a time when the Western countries are so preoccupied with their own internal and external problems that they cannot undertake military commitments in this sub-continent or they find it inadvisable to do so for fear of provoking a world conflict.

Even in the unlikely event of a recrudescence of border fighting between China and India, India could not, considering the mountain terrain, deploy more than three to four divisions against the Chinese. One may justifiably ask, then, why India is doubling the size of her standing army to 22 divisions. Even allowing for the necessary reserves, what are

[6] N. J. Nanpuria, Editor, *Times of India*, April 8, 1963.

the remaining divisions aimed against? The fact of the matter is that, taking advantage of the favorable Western response to her demands for arms, India is planning to raise two armies, one with which to face China and the other to use against Pakistan and her other smaller neighbors in pursuance of her expansionist objectives. It should also be noted that any army meant for China would by the nature of things be so positioned as to be able to wheel round swiftly to attack East Pakistan. Thus both the armies pose a grave threat to this country.

Having built up this enormous war machine, India's leadership would need to justify the great hardships it has imposed on the Indian people in that process. It might also want to regain face which India has lost in the fighting with China. It is possible, therefore, that India might decide to do so—as soon as a suitable opportunity offers itself—by throwing its massive armor against Pakistan, and possibly striking, in the first instance, against that part of Kashmir which is under Pakistan's control but which India claims to be "Indian territory."

It may be recalled in this connection that in the Security Council in 1963, India, while claiming "sovereignty" over the whole of Kashmir, charged that Pakistan was guilty of "continuing aggression" against India so long as she remained in possession of any part of Kashmir. Several prominent Indian leaders have, from time to time, openly urged the use of force to drive Pakistan out of Kashmir.[7] That this demand is not at variance with the official view is apparent from a White Paper, "*Kashmir and the United Nations,*" which was issued by the Government of India when the Kashmir dispute came up before the Security Council in 1962. After stating that "Pakistan continues to occupy half of the Indian Union terri-

[7] Sanjiva Reddy, President of India's ruling party, the Congress, inaugurating its Annual Session on January 4, 1962, stated: "Cease-fire could not be accepted as a permanent solution of the Kashmir problem. The whole country is behind the Government in liberating the one-third of Kashmir which is under Pakistan's illegal occupation." He added: "We hope that within a short period the Government will take steps to liberate that part of Kashmir."

tory of Jammu and Kashmir," the White Paper goes on to say, "Pakistan should vacate this aggression on Indian territory." It then proceeds to warn: "India is prepared to be patient and tolerant and not resort to force to remove Pakistan aggression, but it is obvious that there is a limit to patience and tolerance." Such a warning is open to only one interpretation.

There are other reasons why we apprehend India may launch an aggressive venture against Pakistan. It is well known to students of the sub-continent's history that the Hindus of India were against the creation of a separate homeland for Muslims in the form of Pakistan and, after opposing it tooth and nail for years, gave in because they could not otherwise get rid of the British. Thereafter, while consolidating and building up their own strength, the Indians have let no opportunity pass of weakening and neutralizing Pakistan. The present Indian leadership makes no secret of the fact that it regards Pakistan as "India's enemy number one." It is, therefore, the height of naïveté to say, as one State Department official in Washington said recently, that there is nothing in Pakistan which India wants.

Until the outbreak of fighting with China, and even during most of that fighting, more than three-fourths of India's best-equipped forces remained massed on Pakistan's borders. In December 1962, Mr. Nehru himself admitted that Indian military preparedness had been directed primarily against Pakistan.[8] This still remains India's basic position, and although there have been some changes in the disposition of the Indian forces, the collective strength of those massed on the borders of West Pakistan and East Pakistan remains formidable.

Nor, indeed, would an act of aggression by India be unusual. India has used force time and again to settle her territorial

[8] Explaining the reasons for Indian reverses in the fighting against China, Mr. Nehru said that "most of our military thinking" had been conditioned to the possibility of a war with Pakistan. (Philip Potter, *Baltimore Sun,* December 28, 1962.)

disputes. Let me recall some of these instances. Immediately after independence in 1947, Junagadh, a state with a Muslim ruler, acceded to Pakistan. India strongly protested when she learnt that the ruler contemplated this. In a telegram to the Pakistan Prime Minister, the Indian Prime Minister said that since the population of Junagadh was 80 per cent Hindu and was opposed to accession to Pakistan, the Government of India could not acquiesce in the ruler's decision to accede to Pakistan. They would, however, be willing to accept the verdict of the people of the state on this question, provided the plebiscite was held under the joint supervision of the Indian and Junagadh Governments.[9] Since Pakistan would not agree to this proposition, Indian troops marched into Junagadh and seized it by force.

In the case of Kashmir, on the other hand, Indian logic was conveniently reversed. There, the Indian army marched into the state on the strength of an instrument of "accession" signed by the Hindu Maharaja against the known wishes of the 80 per cent of the people of Kashmir who are Muslims. In fact, at the time the Maharaja signed this document his armies were in retreat against the popular forces and he himself had fled the state capital, Srinagar, and taken refuge in Jammu. It was at that time, when his writ had practically ceased to run in Kashmir, that the Maharaja sought the help of the Indian armed forces. This was promptly offered, but on condition that his state accede to India, whereupon he was prevailed upon to sign an instrument of accession. (It was on the basis of this document that India keeps claiming "sovereignty" over Kashmir.) Thereafter, the Indian forces moved in, took possession of the major part of Kashmir and have held it ever since. A pledge repeatedly given by Mr. Nehru that India would let the people of Kashmir decide the question of accession to India or Pakistan in a free plebiscite still remains to be honored.

[9] Mr. Nehru's telegram dated September 12, 1947.

On September 11, 1948, Quaid-i-Azam Mahomed Ali Jinnah died. The nation was plunged into sorrow over the death of the Founder of Pakistan. India chose that particular moment to march her forces into Hyderabad, another state with a Muslim ruler, and forcibly seized it, not because Hyderabad had wanted to accede to Pakistan, but because it had hesitated somewhat to accede to India.

India again employed the same technique recently to settle her territorial dispute with Portugal over Goa. Within a few weeks of Mr. Nehru's visit to Washington in November 1961, in the course of which he declared that India had "a passion for peace," the Indian army invaded and forcibly annexed Goa. It is interesting also to recall in this connection that on several occasions in the past Mr. Nehru had strongly repudiated any suggestion that India take over Goa by force. On one such occasion, speaking in the Indian Parliament on September 17, 1955, Mr. Nehru said:

> From the very outset our policy, both at home and abroad, has been to solve all problems peacefully. If we ourselves acted against that policy we would be regarded as deceitful hypocrites.

Mr. Nehru could hardly have given a stronger assurance to Goa against a forcible seizure. Nevertheless, when the opportune moment came, those high-sounding declarations were forgotten and another territorial dispute was settled by use of force. What is more, Mr. Nehru's conscience was outraged when the West took unkindly to the Indian grab of Goa. He castigated his critics for "being ignorant of the facts of today and of the past dozen years."[10]

It is because of this background of India's hostility toward Pakistan, her expansionist designs and her aggressive policies that Pakistanis view the continued flow of Western arms into India from their allies with deep dismay and alarm. Indian assurances to the effect that she will not use American arms

---

[10] Mr. Nehru on Mr. Adlai Stevenson's criticism of India's aggression in the Security Council, December 19, 1961.

against Pakistan fail to carry conviction with the people of Pakistan in the light of India's repeated repudiation of her solemn pledges regarding Kashmir and her record of aggression.

Neither do American assurances against the misuse of these weapons reassure our people. They argue that the Indians have thus far successfully got away with every one of their acts of aggression, including that against Goa. Here was aggression against a NATO ally—and neither the United Nations, which was paralyzed by a Soviet veto, nor NATO nor the United States did anything to undo it. If India attacked Pakistan or Pakistan-held Kashmir on the excuse that she was "recovering" what she claims to be "Indian territory," our people fear that the great powers might again be either unwilling to intervene out of consideration for their global policies or unable to thwart Indian aggression.

Apart from the fact that continued Western arms assistance to India causes deep concern in Pakistan and subjects Pakistan's alliance with the West to increasing strain, it is unlikely that it will achieve the objective in view. For if the security and welfare of the Indo-Pakistan subcontinent are the objective, then what is needed is not the injection of massive doses of military aid into India but a rapprochement between India and Pakistan, such as would ensure a disengagement and could even open the way to a reduction of the Indian and Pakistan forces. Such a rapprochement can be brought about only through a just and honorable settlement of the Kashmir dispute. It can be achieved in no other way.

On the other hand, so long as the dispute over Kashmir continues, India-Pakistan tension will continue to mount, immobilizing the bulk of the Indian and Pakistan armies in a senseless confrontation. In such a situation the flow of arms into India would fail to strengthen the sub-continent's defense posture. It would, moreover, make—as indeed it already has made—a resolution of the Kashmir conflict even more difficult.[11] The recent move to integrate occupied Jammu and Kashmir with India, in defiance of the Security Council resolutions, cannot but be regarded as a further manifestation of India's determination to absorb the state irrespective of her international commitments and pledges. All this is going to aggravate India-Pakistan bitterness, heighten their mutual fears and suspicions and force on them an arms race that could spell disaster for both countries. Such an arms race would inevitably necessitate imposition of heavier economic burdens on the peoples of both countries and an even greater diversion of their meagre resources to armament; it would dangerously slow down their already inadequate economic growth rate, create popular discontent and thus make them an easier prey to subversive forces. Surely this could not be the way to promote the security or welfare of the peoples of the sub-continent. A massive Indian military build-up would, further, imperil the existing precarious balance of power in this area. It would increase the existing sense of insecurity among India's smaller neighbors, which could force them to courses of action that might undermine the West's position throughout South Asia.

[11] Since the Birch Grove decision, Mr. Nehru's attitude on Kashmir has been rapidly hardening. His latest stand on this dispute is reflected in his statement in the Indian Parliament on September 3, 1963, to the effect that any change in Kashmir would have "disastrous consequences." (*Times of India,* September 4, 1963.)

II.

Africa
and Asia

A REVIEW*

I N the African continent the most striking phenomenon today is the emergence of a large number of independent countries. The continent still has its problems: for instance, in South Africa, South-West Africa and Southern Rhodesia. But one development has been most encouraging. Although, in comparison with Asia, the African countries had a late start in civilization, culture and religion, as soon as they achieved independence they showed a most commendable initiative. They realized at once that they must look to a future of cooperative living. In this realization, Africa is ahead of Asia. Several conferences have taken place or are about to take place in Africa with the object of evolving a coordinated system of inter-related economic and political assistance and a unanimity of thought on major issues. The newly independent nations of Africa deserve our congratulations.

Turning to Asia, we find that two factors dominate the situation at the moment. First, there is the struggle between the United States and China and, second, there is the clash between India and China.

The situation is very blurred, so far as the struggle between China and the United States is concerned. In the struggle now going on in South Vietnam and Laos, there is no worthwhile military target at all: nothing which one can hit hard and then say: "This problem will now be resolved." The struggle there is for the minds of men. In that part of the world, ever since the Japanese occupation in the last World War, the people have not known peace. The question is: what will win the hearts of the people, the *status quo* or the message of Communism? I believe that by and large the choice confronting mankind is not necessarily between clear cut good or clear cut evil but

* From an address at a press luncheon, London, July 1964.

between varying degrees of evil, and it may well happen that
the Southeast Asian people who have undergone suffering for
20 or more years may say: "If it will bring us peace, let us
have Communism." So I think that the *status quo* forces, which
are in power today, carry a tremendous obligation to win the
hearts of the people and to demonstrate that they can offer
a better future than Communism. Until that battle is won, the
struggle in Southeast Asia will continue.

Again, this struggle can be resolved only if there is some
form of understanding between the United States and China,
and at the moment the chances of such an understanding do
not appear propitious. The possibility of the two sides sitting
round a conference table seems to be remote, and whilst this
situation lasts there is a continuing danger of enlargement of
the struggle. Already, there has been talk of extending the war
from South Vietnam to North Vietnam. Should this ever happen, I have no doubt that the war may become much larger
than is anticipated. Military and political calculations clearly
force one to this conclusion.

Then we have the conflict between China and India. In my
view this conflict could have been avoided. I firmly believe that
the conflict was intended to be a limited struggle designed to
establish, rightly or wrongly, a measure of stability of the
border. I cannot for one moment accept that China can use
Tibet as a base for major operations in the conquest of India.

If there is indeed a plan for the conquest of India by China,
the operational base will have to be somewhere else, and not
Tibet. The average height of the Tibetan plateau is 18,000 feet.
There are three roads running into Tibet: one does not know
the state of these roads. There is talk of a railway being built.
I do not suppose that the roads can be used for more than two
or three months in the year, and if the railway is built its
capacity will not accommodate more than two or three divisions. Our estimate is that not more than 125,000 troops were
stationed in Tibet in October 1962 when the conflict with

India took place. Any suggestion that Tibet can be used to launch a major operation against India is sheer military nonsense. The geography and the logistic problems will not allow it, and if the Chinese forces ever attempt it they will at once be exposed to strong counter-attack. That, indeed, was the reason why there was a cease-fire.

Meanwhile, India is creating an army of one million men at a cost of nearly $1.9 billion. The smaller countries like Pakistan, which have not been on good terms with India, are wondering where this enormous force is going to be used. An inept appreciation of the situation, resulting from the clash between India and China, has led India into embarking upon intolerable military expenditures and creating serious tensions with her smaller neighbors in Asia. I believe that this is a self-defeating policy. If I were an Indian, and even if the threat from China was a reality, I would cut my losses and come to terms with Pakistan. The Indo-Pakistan sub-continent has to be defended as a whole by Pakistan and India, and this cannot be done so long as the armies of the two countries are engaged right in the heart of the sub-continent in a negative effort. During the last 17 years this negativism has drained the blood of India and of Pakistan and has done neither of them any good at all.

PROBLEMS OF FREEDOM*

THE end of the Second World War witnessed an upsurge of the colonial peoples engaged in a desperate struggle to rid themselves of foreign domination. Throughout the length and breadth of Africa and Asia nationalist movements generated among these peoples, a massive resistance to subjugation and overwhelming determination to wrest freedom from alien hands. The hold of colonial Powers began to weaken and finally gave way. As the march of the people started, the victorious echo of their footsteps traveled from country to country, and several sovereign states began to emerge holding aloft the banner of liberty.

There are still a few ramparts of colonialism which have yet to be demolished: their transient existence serves only to remind us of an age which is dead and gone.

Meanwhile, those who have been able to secure their inalienable right to freedom, still continue to pay the heavy toll which a long period of servitude inevitably imposes on a people. They have yet to fill the void in various spheres of life that colonialism has left in its wake. The struggle for freedom for them is, no doubt, over. But there is still another struggle — and perhaps a harder one — ahead of them. This is the struggle to guard closely their hard won freedom and to protect it from the insidious threat of cultural and intellectual subservience.

What use we make of our freedom will depend primarily on how we conduct ourselves in the realm of thought for it is ideas which generate action. Colonialism has bequeathed to us a formidable legacy of problems which we must face and resolve. This requires that we must channelize our emotional impulses into purposeful and constructive endeavors.

* From the inaugural address, Afro-Asian seminar on art, literature and culture, Lahore, February 1965.

Years of toil and perseverance, of constraint and privation, lie ahead of us. The problems of poverty, hunger, disease and illiteracy cannot be resolved by the magic wand of freedom alone. We must carry out a pragmatic probe into our social, economic, political and religious problems and find an answer, based on realism. Each people have their own genius and their own destiny to fulfil. But there are certain human values and principles which are universal and which hold humanity together.

Many of us are new nations only in a technical sense. Our cultures and civilizations date back to times immemorial and have in them good as well as bad elements. To these have also been added both wholesome and unwholesome legacies left behind by foreign domination.

Those among us who lay claim to ancient civilizations are sometimes under the illusion that the lure of Western civilization, based on science and technology, can be resisted by burying their heads in the sands of their past. The ease with which men and ideas travel these days makes it still more difficult to shut oneself in. No country can now remain aloof from world currents, and there is no reason why it should not, irrespective of the source, adopt whatever is good and reject whatever is unwholesome.

It would be to our advantage if we were to identify and retain the basic elements of our own culture and endeavor to synthesize them with the progressive elements offered by other civilizations. Only by effecting such a synthesis can we sustain our individuality and our character, and still enter the age of science and technology to enable us to consolidate our freedom, to raise the standard of living of our peoples and to provide ourselves with a full and satisfying life free from physical want and mental stagnation.

It is easier to swing to the extremes than to attain the wise medium. Those who want to live in the past are often averse to the pain of adopting new ideas. On the other hand, those who shun the past completely do so perhaps because they do not wish to swim upstream; they find it easier to float with the current. Emerging nations must, therefore, think and act independently if they are to maintain their independent existence.

It is particularly in the sphere of religion that the process of adjustment to the scientific and technological age presents a serious problem. Most religions have tended to be shrouded in formalism and dogma, and their exponents have frowned upon attempts to face the challenges of the modern times. This has fostered a growing aversion to religion among the younger generation. I am no expert on religion. But it is my firm belief that the basic principles of religion are immutable and constant; they cannot be changed, and should not be changed. But the application of these principles must conform to the demands of changing circumstances. If this does not happen, religion will lose its hold, and its followers will fail to keep pace with forces of advancement.

We must recognize that human beings are by nature traditionalists. And, perhaps, it is good up to a point that they are so. For it helps them to maintain touch with the past so as to deal intelligently with the present and prepare wisely for the future. But traditionalism is of two kinds. One kind is born of inertia and bred by timidity. The other kind does not exclude consciousness of a better way of life. It is the first kind of traditionalism against which we have particularly to guard ourselves, for it is essentially the product of resistance to the use of the faculty of thought. While it is the faculty of thinking which distinguishes man from other forms of animals, it is curious that many human beings are loathe to use it. That is why we witness the amazing spectacle throughout human history that those who have dared to think originally have invariably roused opposition and have been assailed by inveterate objectors. They have been subjected to virulent criticism and branded as heretics. But in the end they have come to be venerated for their positive contribution to human civilization.

The strong desire of the emerging nations to consolidate their independence and to find their true place in life cannot be realized unless there is a period of sustained peace. For it is only in an atmosphere of peace, free from turmoil and conflict, that they can catch up with the time they have lost under alien bondage.

Rising tension between some developing nations and some major Powers, between small countries and their big neighbors, continues to pose a serious threat to world peace. This threat is at once a challenge and an opportunity for the United Nations.

All of us are deeply concerned over the future of the United Nations as an institution designed to work for the lessening of tensions in the world. Inspite of its many limitations, and we in Pakistan have suffered on account of them, the United Nations continues to serve as a forum for the expression of the views of the smaller nations in an endeavor to influence world opinion. It is to be hoped that this organization will yet be enabled to pursue, more effectively, its objective of maintaining world peace and goodwill. If the United Nations were to disintegrate, the major Powers may be able to adjust themselves to the new situation, but the voice of the smaller nations will be lost in the wilderness.

III.

The
Kashmir Dispute

KASHMIR UPHEAVAL *

O   UR hearts are heavy and our feelings hurt over the
        tragic events of the past few months. These events were
        preceded by more than a year of acute anxiety for us
over the massive arms build-up in India on the pretext of the
Chinese threat which nobody believes in now. Whatever India
does in pursuit of her preparations for war concerns us so
long as she poses a threat to us.

The systematic eviction of Indian Muslims from Assam
and Tripura, in spite of our protests and regardless of our
requests for talks at the Ministerial level, has been a running
sore, poisoning the already strained relations between the
two countries.

The announcement that India was planning to absorb the
state of Jammu and Kashmir,[1] in disregard of international
obligations, came as a further shock to us. That it was the last
straw which broke the back of the long-suffering people of
Jammu and Kashmir is proved by the upheaval which shook
the state during the last month.

This upheaval was set in motion by the mysterious theft
of the holy relic from the Hazratbal shrine[2] which injured the
religious susceptibilities not only of the Muslims of occupied
Kashmir but also of Pakistan. Subsequent events have, however, shown that the agitation was due also to the resentment
of the people of Jammu and Kashmir at their continued subjugation by India and at the Indian design to integrate their
state.

Foreign observers, the few who managed to enter the state
while it was aflame, have reported that the agitation was not

* From a broadcast, February 1964.
[1] On October 3, 1963, the Prime Minister of India-occupied Kashmir dis-
closed a directive "to bring Kashmir closer" to India. On November 27,
1963, the Indian Home Minister announced the "Integration" plan before
Parliament.
[2] December 27, 1963.

merely over the loss of the holy relic; it was an open rebellion against the tyrannical regimes imposed upon the state and, what is more, against India herself.

Even a person like Bakhshi Ghulam Mohammad[3] had to admit publicly that the people are demanding not only a proper identification of the recovered relic and the release of Sheikh Abdullah,[4] but also a free and fair plebiscite. Public demands for the withdrawal of the Indian army of occupation and for the state's accession to Pakistan have penetrated the iron curtain drawn around occupied Kashmir.

These events and demands have made it clear to friend and foe, and shall I say to neutrals too, that Indian arms and money have not been able to break the will of the people of Jammu and Kashmir who have registered a vote against the Indian hold over their state in what virtually has been a spontaneous referendum.

It is because of this unequivocal expression of the wishes of the people of Jammu and Kashmir that we have considered it necessary to remind the Security Council that its repeated resolutions for holding a free and fair plebiscite, resolutions to which India herself is a party, must now be implemented. The voice of the people of Jammu and Kashmir can no longer be ignored.

The Indian intention to integrate the state of Jammu and Kashmir with India, despite a clear Security Council resolution to the contrary, creates a new and critical situation and constitutes defiance of the Security Council which must be seriously considered by that body.

Without a resolution of the Kashmir problem, there will be no peace in this region. For the hearts of the people of Paki-

[3] Prime Minister 1953-63; arrested September 22, 1964.
[4] Prime Minister 1947-53; deposed and arrested by order of Indian Government August 9, 1953; released January 8, 1958; rearrested April 30, 1958; released April 8, 1964.

stan beat as one with those of their brethren in Jammu and Kashmir. Seldom have I seen our people so agitated as now over the sufferings of their brethren in the state who stood in hundreds of thousands in the streets for nearly a fortnight, day and night, in biting cold and snow, to take part in what was described by India as merely a religious agitation but is now known to be a mass demand for the promised plebiscite as well.

The happenings in Kashmir so deeply stirred Pakistan that, in far off Khulna in East Pakistan, there was a burst of public disorder because the people's emotions got the better of their reason. I am glad that the authorities took firm measures and restored order within a short time. It is unfortunate that this minor incident should have been used as an excuse for staging a carnage of Muslims in Calcutta and in other districts of West Bengal.

Foreign newspapers have described this carnage as an "anti-Muslim rampage by mobs of Hindus." Very large numbers of Indian Muslims have already sought refuge in Pakistan. I have pointed out in a letter to the President of India that the Hindu mobs of Calcutta must have taken their cue from the Government's systematic eviction earlier of the Indian Muslims from Assam and Tripura.

I do not wish to condone the consequential rioting in Dacca district. The Government has suppressed it as firmly as possible. The police, the East Pakistan Rifles and the army were all called out to control effectively the sporadic disorder which broke out in unexpected places. And I would like to make it clear that we propose to curb disorder wherever it might occur.

I appeal to my people not to let their emotions get the better of their good sense. The sight of one's brethren, robbed and driven out of their hearths and homes, is certainly most upsetting. But it is no solution of the problem to beat up or drive out other innocent persons who constitute the minority community in our country. It is not just nor fair that innocent people should be made to pay for what their co-religionists have done in India. Let us behave like a civilized people even if others don't.

We must provide relief to the Indian Muslims who have been robbed and driven out. I have heard glowing accounts of how our people rose to the occasion and shared their food and clothing with the Muslim refugees from India.

But the real solution of the problem is that law and order must be maintained and complete security must be ensured to the minority community in both the countries so that the refugees can go back to their homes, to their lands and trades. We are resolved to do this on our side. And I would like to assure the minority communities in Pakistan that we will use all the resources of the state to provide them full security and freedom to pursue their avocations and their faith.

Against the few communal disturbances in Pakistan during the last 16 years, there have been well over 500 communal riots in India. That this should happen in so-called secular India, in the land which claims to be the home of non-violence, passes one's comprehension.

I would like sober-minded Indians to ponder over this record. To oppress a weak minority reflects no credit on the majority community. It is a blot on any civilized nation.

It is not too late even now. If the majority community in India were to make a genuine effort to treat Muslims as equal citizens, and to give them security, it would find that the 50 to 60 million Indian Muslims are a source of strength to them. India has enough of everything to make her prosperous and great without having to expel the minority community. Why is it being victimized and persecuted? What good can come to India through such action?

So far as the state of Jammu and Kashmir is concerned, world opinion, expressed through the Security Council of the world organization, has refused to recognize India's hold over that state. Defiance of world opinion does not add to the prestige or good name of India. It weakens her position in international relations. She has had to sink tens of millions of rupees to hold down the state. But all the millions of rupees, all the armies and the puppet governments imposed on the state to break the will of the people, have failed to make an impression on the people of Jammu and Kashmir who are now in open revolt.

Would continued suppression be of any avail? Certainly not. Neither the people of Jammu and Kashmir nor the people of Pakistan will rest content until the former are allowed to exercise their right freely to choose which country they wish to join. India has more than once promised to let this happen. Why not honor that promise?

Would to God that India would have peace for herself, and let us have peace too. We both need it for the social and economic development of our peoples. If that development suffers, the consequences will be dire and far-reaching.

I thought that the Indians were a businesslike people and knew how to draw up a balance-sheet. Is the forced occupation of a small state worth the international disgrace involved in repudiating solemn pledges? Is it worth the billions that India has already spent and will continue to spend on keeping the state down by force? Is it worth incurring Pakistan's hostility, when her friendship would have been a source of strength to India? Is it worth neglecting the socio-economic development of India's teeming millions? Is there no person in India who can draw up a balance-sheet and tell his Government that this is a heavily losing, in fact disastrous, business for India?

Now that the people of Jammu and Kashmir have made

their wishes known in unmistakable terms, let India show her statesmanship by honoring her international pledges. If she does not do so, the Security Council must ensure that its solemn resolutions, reached after much deliberation, are implemented. This is a test case for the Security Council because the problem has defied solution so long, because there will be no peace in this region unless it is resolved, and because it can be resolved easily if India is made to fulfill her solemn pledges.

If the Security Council fails to enforce its carefully considered resolutions, then I am afraid the United Nations will go the way of the League of Nations. What was wrong with the latter except that the issues which came before it were decided according to the dictates of power politics and not according to the principles of impartial justice? What is right must be supported and enforced. What is wrong must be denied and rectified. Otherwise, no order or peace can obtain.

The United Nations is the last hope for international peace. If it fails, the prospect would be horrifying, for we will go back to the law of the jungle. It will not fail if it judges the issues before it on moral grounds of what is right or wrong, irrespective of who are involved. I hope that this will happen in all cases including that of Jammu and Kashmir.

In the meanwhile, I ask my people to be patient. They have been so hitherto. Patience is a difficult virtue to observe but it is one of the highest. The Holy Quran is full of repeated commands to be patient in adversity. The down-trodden people of Jammu and Kashmir are awakening and standing up to their unwanted masters against very heavy odds. They have won the admiration, not only of their brethren in Pakistan, but also of the people of the whole world for their courage, steadfastness and restraint in their trials and tribulations. I hope that there will soon be an end to their misery and subjugation.

KASHMIR AND PEACE*

THE peace of the Indo-Pakistan sub-continent is threatened by the Jammu and Kashmir dispute. Recent events have made the situation highly explosive. India has used over one hundred thousand soldiers to hold down this small state. But even this show of force no longer intimidates the brave people of Jammu and Kashmir, who have risen in revolt against India's proposed integration of the state. In spite of ruthless suppression and strict censorship, the whole world knows the truth by now.

All foreign observers have reported that the people of Jammu and Kashmir are clamoring for the long promised right of self-determination and for accession to Pakistan.

The Indian newspapers were allowed by the Government of India only to say that the people of Jammu and Kashmir were asking for the removal of the oppressive and corrupt state government. This technique has been used by the Indian rulers in the past to divert attention from the truth and to prepare the ground for the dismissal of unwanted state governments. True to form, the Shamsuddin[1] government has been sacked. Nemesis has overtaken this short-lived government for dismissing a large number of Muslim officers from service because of their alleged sympathy for the pro-Pakistan movement in the state. Officers from India are now to be appointed to key posts in Jammu and Kashmir. Change of governments, or change of officers, is not going to make the slightest difference to the resolve of the people of Jammu and Kashmir to

---

* From a broadcast, March 1964.
[1] Mr. Shamsuddin was installed by the Government of India as Prime Minister of the state of Jammu and Kashmir on October 12, 1963. He was replaced on February 28, 1964.

assert their right of self-determination. Nor would it make any difference to our determination to secure for the people of the state a proper opportunity for the exercise of this right.

The recent Security Council debate has shown that the overwhelming majority of members of the Council rejected the Indian plea that all was well with the state, that there was no case for action by the Security Council and that the Kashmir dispute was a closed chapter. It is amazing how India has changed her ground from time to time before this august body. And it is amazing how arguments, which merely echo the hollowness of the Indian case, are used with an air of false assurance and without a qualm of conscience.

It is in the interest of India as well as of Pakistan to resolve their differences with good grace. India has pleaded that if a plebiscite is held in Jammu and Kashmir, it will lead to communal disturbances in India. Why should that happen? Would the mere holding of the plebiscite provoke the Indian Hindu majority into rioting? If that is so, can India claim that she is treating her minorities as full citizens? Or are the minorities in India hostages on whom India can wreak vengeance for what their co-religionists may do outside or even inside India?

India knows, and the whole world should know, that there are many non-Muslims in Kashmir who demand a plebiscite. So this is not a communal question. India says that Hindus will have to leave the state if Kashmir decided to join Pakistan as a result of the plebiscite, and that communal disturbances will take place in India. This is an admission that the plebiscite will go against India, although India's alleged fear of communal rioting is imaginary. But even if there is some substance in this fear, is it just that because some hooligans in India may get out of control millions of people in Jammu and Kashmir should be denied their right to self-determination? The holding of a plebiscite in the Sylhet district[2] (in

2 July 13, 1947.

present East Pakistan) or in the former North West Frontier Province[3] prior to independence did not lead to communal disturbances.

·Is the powerful Government of India, now armed to the teeth, unable to maintain law and order in its own country? This bogey of communal disturbances following a plebiscite in Jammu and Kashmir is a terrible admission by the Government of India of its inability to discharge the elementary responsibility of maintaining order within its territory.

I can assure India and the Security Council, in the name of the people of Pakistan, that if a fair and free plebiscite is held in Jammu and Kashmir, and if the people of that state decide to join India, there will be no communal repercussions in Pakistan.

The Security Council and resolutions of the United Nations Commission for India and Pakistan requiring the holding of a plebiscite in Jammu and Kashmir were accepted by India and Pakistan. India now seeks to repudiate them. She has successfully defied these resolutions so far. Compare this situation with what India herself thinks of the defiance of the United Nations when another country is involved. Speaking on the Congo problem in 1961, the Indian representative said:

> I would like to ask if the Republic of Congo, which is a member state at the present time, is going to say to us that it will not permit the implementation of the United Nations resolutions. Then is this a state of complete hostility between one member state and the whole of the United Nations?

If the Republic of Congo could be condemned in such strong terms for one fault, what is the verdict of the world on India's repeated default to implement the resolutions of the United Nations? Is this not a case of unprecedented hostility between one member state and the whole of the United

[3] July 20, 1947.

Nations? And if the United Nations tolerates it or connives at it, then will not the United Nations lose its authority and effectiveness?

APPEAL TO REASON*

OUR hearts go out to our brethren in occupied Jammu and Kashmir who are passing through a most difficult, and what might be the most decisive, time of their life. Years of armed occupation and suppression have failed to still the voice of freedom which has now burst forth as a mighty and anguished roar whose echoes have been heard far beyond the hills of Jammu and Kashmir. Strict censorship has not succeeded in preventing foreign and neutral observers from reporting to the world that the people of the state are now in open rebellion against India and that they wish to exercise their right of self-determination, a right which was promised and promised again and again to them, but which was never fulfilled. That the voice of the people of Jammu and Kashmir has been heard by the world was clear in the Security Council debates where we found countries of Asia, Africa and the West endorsing the demand of the people of Jammu and Kashmir for self-determination. Even outside the Security Council we have received valuable support from our friends and neighbors in our resolve to secure the expeditious implementation of the United Nations resolutions dealing with the Kashmir dispute.

I know that the postponement[1] of the Kashmir debate in the Security Council must have caused deep disappointment to the people of Jammu and Kashmir. We will not relax our efforts, in spite of these delays, as we know that the people of Jammu and Kashmir will not relax theirs. The resolution publicly passed on March 15 last by the Action Committee, admittedly the most representative body of the people of the state today, is a declaration of human rights for the people of

* From a broadcast, April 1964.
[1] At India's request the U. N. Security Council adjourned its deliberations on Kashmir on March 20, 1964.

Jammu and Kashmir. It places on record, in most unmistakable terms, that the people of Jammu and Kashmir will not rest content until a free and fair plebiscite has been held. That this resolution was passed under the shadow of Indian bayonets shows the spirit and courage of the people. And they are fortunate to have among them selfless and devoted leaders who will not be lured by promises of personal gain or cowed down by threats.

I earnestly appeal to the Government of India to realize how futile it is to continue to suppress the people of Jammu and Kashmir. The best or the worst that India could do in this direction has failed in its purpose. The India-installed puppet governments in Kashmir which are becoming demonstrably weaker in popular appeal, or Indian measures such as the projected integration of the state, are not going to retrieve a situation which is now beyond redemption. Bigger armies will break the back of the Indian economy but not the will of the people of Jammu and Kashmir or our resolve.

Let men of good sense and statesmanship in India advise their Government to take the obviously honorable course of settling the Kashmir dispute by holding the promised plebiscite. It is amazing how a resolve to do the right thing can, at one stroke, solve many problems. An honorable way out of the present situation exists. And it is not difficult to take it.

NEED FOR REALISM *

THE release of Sheikh Abdullah,[1] whose spirit remains undaunted, is a victory for the people of Jammu and Kashmir. During the recent agitation, the people of the state demanded three things. First, the recovery of the sacred relic. The agitation was so intense that the Government of India had to go all out to trace the stolen relic. Let us hope that the recovered relic is a genuine one, although the mystery about the culprits responsible for the theft remains unsolved.

The second demand was for the release of Sheikh Abdullah. If this has been conceded, it is because the Government of India realized that it had no alternative. The farce of the so-called conspiracy case against the Sheikh could not be continued any more. And popular agitation for the Sheikh's release could not be ignored or suppressed. Those in India who take a poor view of their Government's action in releasing him are not aware of the true state of things in the Valley. The Government of India would not have invited unnecessary criticism if it had told the truth to its people. Unfortunately, even the reports of the foreign observers were blacked out by the Indian press and radio.

The third and the most vital demand of the people is for self-determination. Now that the other two demands have been conceded, there is reason to hope that New Delhi may yield to this demand also.

The winds of change are blowing all over the world. The non-official delegations from Pakistan which went to Europe, Africa, the Middle East and Southeast Asia to discuss the Kashmir situation created an extremely favorable atmosphere in the countries visited. Most of these countries have come out openly in favor of self-determination for the people of

* From a broadcast, May 1964.
[1] April 8, 1964.

Jammu and Kashmir. The Security Council, by an overwhelming majority, has endorsed the right.

There are men of goodwill and courage in India who realize that there will be no real peace and no real progress in this sub-continent until the Kashmir dispute is settled in a fair and honorable manner and until Hindus and Muslims live in amity and friendship rather than in enmity and hate.

Leaders of India also admit now that recent communal orgies in that country were not stray incidents or reprisals against what allegedly happened in Pakistan. They were well-planned and well-organized efforts to stir up widespread communal turbulence. Even the educated classes among Hindus were infected by communal virus, so much so that they took an active part in rioting. And the police stood by or joined the rioters. The virus has reached the vitals of India.

As I see it, there is a two-pronged attack on the Muslim minority in India. On the one hand, the state Governments of Assam, Tripura and West Bengal, on the pretext of Pakistani infiltration, are evicting Muslims on a large scale. On the other, organized militant communal parties in India are doing their utmost to make the life of Indian Muslims impossible.

The ruthless extermination of Muslims by militant Hindu organizations is designed to liquidate the Muslims of India, to create refugee rehabilitation problems for Pakistan, and to ensure that no workable arrangement for co-existence between India and Pakistan can be made.

The much harassed Indian Muslims are not demanding economic or social benefits, or improvement of employment facilities which have been denied to them. All they seem to be asking for is to be left alone. All they seem to be worrying about is how to save their skins.

The heart of the problem will remain untouched until India realizes the value of living at some measure of peace with Pakistan. There is need for realism in India and need for a change in thinking. When that happens the communal and other problems that bedevil relations between the two countries will find their correct perspective and will be freed of emotionalism, allowing reason to prevail.

CRITICAL JUNCTURE *

ON behalf of the people of Pakistan, as well as on mine, I convey to the people of India our sincere condolences on their great national loss. We share their grief over the death of Prime Minister Jawaharlal Nehru.

An event of such tragic magnitude should be an occasion for searching of hearts by all those ordained by God to direct human affairs. Those placed in positions of authority and control over human destiny carry a grave responsibility. They have the opportunity and the power to do immense good or incalculable harm. The consequences of how they act can no longer be confined to their own spheres of action but must extend to others. For the nations of the world are now so closely inter-linked that the affairs of one have repercussions on the fate of many.

We commiserate with India in her hour of sorrow and we extend a warm hand of friendship to the people of India across the borders. Today may be the day for both sides, in particular for the new leadership in India, to take a fresh look at our relationship. On our part, we shall readily respond to a sincere move for the improvement of Indo-Pakistan relations.

The bitterness and recriminations which have gone on for nearly 17 years between India and Pakistan have done no good to either side. They have only caused much human misery and suffering, apart from incalculable loss in material terms.

Hatred and anger fan the fires of hell in human minds. Why not put them out? It is nobler and more conducive to one's own happiness to live on terms of friendliness with others.

India and Pakistan are neighbors, for better or for worse. Why let it be for the worse? Why not try the alternative of living together for the better?

* From a broadcast, June 1964.

We both have within our countries communities professing different faiths. They could hate and fight one another. They could also, with a little self-control, learn to be tolerant of one another. This is not a task beyond human capacity. For a civilized and organized society the way to greatness with honor lies in forbearance and discipline.

There are undoubtedly differences between India and ourselves. It would not be realistic if we were to ignore them. What is required is a disposition to face and solve these differences. Look at the history of the European countries which, till recently, were the worst enemies of one another. And think of the human suffering their enmity led to—not only for themselves but for the world as a whole. Yet, today, they are organizing themselves into a community of close and friendly nations. Instead of trying to destroy one another, they are strengthening themselves. The material advantages, for which most of the wars took place fruitlessly, have now been gained by them by composing their differences and by forgetting decades of past hatred. Those little bits of territory for which they fought with such grievous consequences no longer seem to matter. The differences and disputes which looked so intractable and insoluble at one time have vanished as if by a magic wand. That magic wand was nothing but a change of heart. Hatred and enmity were replaced by friendship and good neighborliness. And the gains have been incalculable.

It should be easier for India and Pakistan to resolve their differences because both need peace and security to develop their countries and improve the lot of their teeming millions. Herein lies our future. And not in preparing for war with each other, which wastes human and economic resources even if no war takes place.

The major irritant in Indo-Pakistan relations is the Kashmir dispute. Everyone knows that the dispute exists. It cannot be just wished away. It would be realistic and statesmanlike to face it and resolve it. It has been festering our relations for too long.

It is vital to settle this issue on an equitable basis and without delay, for the people of Kashmir will not wait indefinitely. The eyes of the world are on us. And if we can come to a sensible settlement, we shall have made a historic contribution to world peace. And its effect will be electric, not only in international councils and affairs, but also on the minds of our own peoples.

We must remove the morbid fear that a settlement of this dispute will jeopardize the position of minorities. On the contrary, I believe that the Kashmir dispute is responsible for agitating communal passions which will disappear once the dispute is settled. It requires courage and statesmanship to cut this gordian knot. The good it will do will far outweigh the loss, if any. It will provide the minorities in both countries with a feeling of relief and a breath of reassurance. No organized or civilized government can treat a section of its people as hostages. To my mind it is not beyond human ingenuity to work out an arrangement whereby the position of the minorities can be fully secured and safeguarded.

The Muslim minority in India, at the time of partition, placed its trust in the good sense and decency of the majority community. Given the chance, it could offer great strength and benefit to India. No person who considers the situation coolly can believe that Indian Muslims constitute a threat to the security of India. That country has been well served by those Muslims whom she gave a chance to serve.

The moral and international stature and strength of India depend on an understanding with Pakistan. Material advantages are also bound to accrue. To mention one advantage, the crushing burden of India's military budget could be reduced by half immediately.

I hope that good sense will yet prevail and that the relations between the two countries will improve to the advantage of both.

FRESH APPROACH*

WHATEVER differences have arisen between Hindus and Muslims were due to the nature of the political struggle at the turn of the century. Once independence was achieved, we should have endeavored to live as good neighbors, in self-interest if not from higher moral considerations. Hostility between India and Pakistan has already caused incalculable damage to both countries. But it is not too late to prevent the situation from deteriorating further. It will require a major effort but that effort must be made if we have to save our countries from disaster.

To begin with we must put a stop to incidents along our borders. What good can these pin-pricks do? They result in senseless loss of innocent human life and produce nothing but bitterness and resentment.

Second, the Indian Muslims must not be exposed to mob rule and constant communal pressures. They are citizens of India and have served her well. Their future is inextricably woven with the future of India, and India's destiny is their destiny. It is for the Government and the people of India to protect the members of the Muslim minority and to give them a sense of belonging to the country. On our part, we regard the minorities in Pakistan as a sacred trust.

I very much hope that the new leadership in India will realize the gravity of allowing free play to communal passions. The minorities in both countries wish to live in peace. And we wish to live in peace with India. Any steps which the new leadership in India may take in this direction will find us willing to meet them more than halfway.

To any impartial and fair-minded observer it should be clear that the injustice done to the people of Jammu and

* From a broadcast, July 1964.

Kashmir must be put right as soon as possible. The whole sub-continent was divided on the principle of communal majority areas. And there is no reason why a departure from this principle should be made in the case of Jammu and Kashmir. The price which India has paid for retaining forcibly the state of Jammu and Kashmir is highly disproportionate to any advantage which she may have gained. And she will continue to pay this price unless she comes to terms over Kashmir. Already a crushing defense burden is leading to inflation, with all its evil consequences, in India. India can halve her defense expenditures with one stroke if she were to settle the Kashmir dispute. What she is spending on Jammu and Kashmir is not only the fabulous sums provided for purchasing the goodwill of the people but also nearly $950 million annually on the unnecessary doubling of her armed forces because of this dispute. There is nothing esoteric about these calculations. The people of India ought to know or be told the details of this wasteful expenditure which is inflicting avoidable sufferings on them.

IV.   India's Military
                     Build-Up

ARMING INDIA*

I HAVE held lengthy discussions with my experts and advisers on the situation that has arisen as a result of the recent conflict betwen our two neighbors, China and India, and its repercussions on our security and relationships.

I have also received communications on the subject from the President of the United States, the Prime Minister of the United Kingdom and the Prime Minister of India.

Broadly speaking, we are seriously disturbed that differences between India and China have erupted into an armed conflict. However, we believe that the scope of this conflict, because of the terrain over which it is being waged, must perforce be limited. Had it been designed otherwise, the contestants would have started the conflict with a considerable campaigning period ahead of them. It would not have been started in October when, in a few weeks, weather conditions would have inevitably brought military operations to a halt.

However unfortunate the present situation, we hope that our two neighbors will be able to settle their problems peacefully and amicably.

Our policy has been based on peace at large, especially peace with our neighbors. Unfortunately, we have so far failed to achieve this with our neighbor, India, because of her unwillingness to reach an equitable and honorable settlement over Kashmir. The result is that we both are wasting on military preparations resources sorely needed for the amelioration of the condition of our peoples. I hope it is still not too late for India to realize the good that will follow a settlement of our differences.

* From a statement, Rawalpindi, November 1962.

From all accounts, a large amount of military equipment is being rushed to India from the United States, the United Kingdom and elsewhere. This may have the effect of enlarging and prolonging the conflict between China and India and, also, add to the serious concern already existing in the minds of our people that these weapons may well be used against us in the absence of an overall settlement with India.

MASSIVE BUILD-UP*

A DEVELOPMENT of immediate concern to us has been the arming of India by the Western countries and the USSR. India has declared a state of emergency to enable the Government to assume dictatorial powers. She has increased her own warlike preparations as if a major war was on.

These preparations are said to be directed against China. Yet China declared a cease-fire unilaterally and withdrew her forces from the conquered territory in December 1962, when the Indian army was on the run and the whole of the Assam plain lay at the victor's feet. And China has since asked for negotiations for a peaceful settlement.

That there is no possibility of a major war between India and China is accepted even in the capitals of those countries which are rushing arms aid to India. Then why are they doing so? The reasons are best known to them. But we can see that they presumably wish to take advantage of anti-China feeling in India to align her to the West or, at least, to range her against China. In this they are sadly mistaken. China and India are the giants of Asia. They know that they will destroy each other if there is a major war. So, a hot war is out of the question. Even a cold war between these giants will be harmful to their interests, politically as well as economically. It will neutralize them completely. And they are sensible enough to know this.

The Indian press has said that the West should not expect India to align herself with the aid givers or to range herself against China.

I am certain that India will, sooner or later, come to terms with China. She has kept the Colombo proposals on the peg. And according to a press report,[1] an emissary of the Indian

* From a broadcast, October 1963.
[1] The *Baltimore Sun,* September 11, 1963.

Prime Minister to the United States has suggested that the United States and the USSR should make a joint statement asking China to initiate talks for a peaceful settlement of the Sino-Indian boundary dispute. The Indian press is also urging a peaceful settlement with China.

Those who are striving to build India against China are going to be disappointed and disillusioned. If present warlike preparations go on in India, her leaders will have to justify the expenditure of nearly $1.9 billion a year on these preparations to the nation which is groaning under heavy taxation and inflation. If the Indian military build-up continues, what would be more natural than a war of conquest by India against her smaller neighbors? And we head the list. We have, therefore, every reason to protest and to feel anxious. And I believe that other small nations in Asia have similar cause to complain. In our case, things have already begun to happen on the Assam-Tripura border where Muslims, who have lived there for generations, who appear on India's voters' list and are Indian citizens, are being driven into Pakistan at the point of bayonet in hapless condition, after being robbed of all their belongings. The reason is simple: The influx of Muslims expelled from India will add heavily to the burdens of Pakistan, a consummation nearest to the Indian heart.

A PERIOD OF ANXIETY*

L OOKING back on the past 18 months, we can see that
we have passed through a period of great anxiety because
of the arms aid secured by India on the pretext of threat
of Chinese aggression. It is now recognized on all hands that
China has no designs to invade India.

India knows, and the whole world knows, that she is
not going to fight China either. For India to wage war against
China will lead to no fruitful result; it may only entail further
disasters for her. And India is shrewd enough to know this.
It is, therefore, a question of time before India comes to a
settlement with China. Meanwhile, the Chinese bug-bear helps
the present rulers of India in several ways. It consolidates and
strengthens their weakening hold on the country. It helps the
Indian Government to obtain the political support of the
Western countries and even of the USSR. Last, but not the
least, it helps the Indian Government to obtain heavy financial
and military aid, again both from the Western countries and
the USSR.

But what will happen when India comes to terms with
China, as she is bound to do? How will she justify to her own
people the extremely heavy burden of maintaining a huge
modern Army, Navy and Air Force? Inflation has already
set in in India, and prices are soaring as a result of warlike
preparations. The present Indian expenditures on defense will
increase, and not decrease, in future years as these preparations get into full swing. It is customary for warlords to
undertake campaigns of conquest to justify expenditures on
acquisition of military strength. Because of the partition of
the sub-continent, and our refusal to accept the integration
of the state of Jammu and Kashmir with India, we stand in

* From a broadcast, January 1964.

the greatest danger of being subjected to Indian aggression. The other countries of this region, which are weaker than India, are naturally and equally perturbed by this development.

The arming of India has emboldened her to announce plans to integrate the state of Jammu and Kashmir. We have said repeatedly that we object in the strongest possible terms to this high-handed violation of solemn international pledges. The arms build-up in India will make no difference to our stand on the Jammu and Kashmir question. We are determined to secure to the people of Jammu and Kashmir their rightful freedom to choose which country they wish to join.

Barring our relations with our Indian neighbor, the last year saw an improvement of our relations with our other neighbors: China, the Soviet Union, Afghanistan, Nepal, Burma and Ceylon. I can only express the hope that world opinion, and the saner elements in India, will assert themselves and make the Indian Government come to a reasonable and honorable settlement with us. If not, the arming of India and her aggressive action in proposing to integrate Jammu and Kashmir will continue to pose a serious threat to our security.

THE CHOICE*

THE Indian trump card in the recent Security Council debate[1] was to raise the bogey of China. Make India strong, it was pleaded, to meet the danger from China. That there is no danger to India from China is now admitted by even those who once spoke about it with conviction. But suppose that there, in fact, was a threat of invasion of the sub-continent by China, would India be in a stronger position if she were on terms of peace and friendship with Pakistan or if the two countries were at daggers drawn and the majority of the Indian army was poised against Pakistan, as has been the position since 1947? It is because of India's refusal to settle the Kashmir dispute that she is now planning to develop and maintain two defense forces: the original force, modernized and strengthened, poised as a direct threat to Pakistan, and the new force, supposed to be required against China, but so deployed that it can at any time be used against Pakistan.

Students of history know that the Indo-Pakistan sub-continent was invaded by outsiders whenever there was internal strife in the region. To differences between India and Pakistan over Kashmir has now been added the revolt of the people of the state itself against unwanted masters. I am convinced that a people, once roused, cannot be suppressed indefinitely. Is this triangular internal strife going to help the defense of this sub-continent? And how long will India's economy be able to bear the crushing burden of two defense forces and of a war budget, which is bound to increase as time goes on? The dead weight of wasteful extravagance will drag India down with her teeming but starving millions. The resulting chaos will be an ideal breeding ground for public discontent and upheaval. Those who wish to save India from disaster

* From a broadcast, March 1964.
[1] February 1964.

should counsel reduction of expenditure on wasteful war
preparations and diversion of resources to social and economic development of India's poverty-stricken millions. Does
it make sense to encourage India to live on a war basis when
we all know that there is no threat of war against her unless
it is of her own making? Where is the need for sinking billions of dollars in India, particularly since she may come
to terms with China at any time, as Prime Minister Lal
Bahadur Shastri hinted recently?

To those who wish to build up India against China, I
repeat the warning that they are going to be let down as they
have been let down previously in other places and by other
leadership. India will and must come to a peaceful settlement
with China after she has fully exploited the present situation.
Although China has no designs against India and wishes to
settle her boundary dispute by peaceful negotiation, let us
assume for the sake of argument that the Indian propaganda
is correct and such designs exist. In that case, the way India
is planning to win her struggle against China is not the right
way. The back-breaking economic burdens on the Indian
people will in the end turn out to be to the advantage of the
aggressor, if any. Why can't this simple logic be understood
by the rulers of India? Must they continue to play a reckless
game to the detriment of their own people and to the detriment of the whole of Asia? If there is a struggle in Asia, it
will not be the peoples of Asia who will be the beneficiaries.

The exploitation of her boundary dispute with China is
another instance of Indian opportunism. It is now well known
that the hold of the Congress party over India is weakening.
The phony emergency in India has helped the present leadership to enforce stringent laws and to regain its hold over the
country. It suits the Government of India to continue the
so-called emergency and to rule the country with extraordinary
measures. The emergency is also bringing India handsome
returns in the form of heavy economic and military aid. It

has secured for India some political support from unexpected quarters. All these may be immediate gains. But this artificial state of things cannot last.

I doubt if the people of the United States realize the cost to them of recent policies. I do not mean simply the financial cost, for this is known, at least to the Government of the United States. What I mean is the damage to the image of the American nation in the eyes of the peoples, at least in Asia. That image has been that the American people invariably championed moral and rightful causes. This image is now in danger of being gravely compromised. We now see that the United States Government is being forced to support, or connive at, India's immoral policies. Should America's great image be damaged in the process, the loss will be irreparable.

V.   Economic Development

EMERGING PATTERNS*

THE dawn of political independence came to Pakistan after a long period of waiting and sacrifice. Pakistanis naturally look forward now to a life of dignity and well-being which was hitherto denied to them. In this atmosphere of high expectations Pakistan, as well as the other Afro-Asian countries, face problems which are similar in character.

Our main problem is to achieve socio-economic growth in as short a time as possible. This task is difficult enough in all conscience but it is made more difficult by our all too meagre resources in money and trained man-power.

Per capita income in Afro-Asian countries is extremely low, and the vast majority of our peoples live a life beset with hunger, disease and ignorance.

The literacy rate is so low that the task of reaching the people and persuading them to change their methods and techniques of work becomes formidable.

The means of communication exist mostly in primitive forms.

Altogether, we lack the infrastructure essential for the attainment of self-sustaining growth.

Our enormous task is made still more difficult sometimes by conditions of political instability and, in the case of most of us, by the alarming growth of population.

The rise in population is of such dimensions that it will neutralize whatever progress we expect to achieve through the mobilization of our modest resources.

These are some of our major internal problems and our common legacies. On top of these, we have some external problems which balk our path towards economic emancipation. They call for an urgent solution.

* From the inaugural address, Afro-Asian Economic Conference, Karachi, December 1963.

Externally, our task is made difficult by some of the policies of developed countries which have accepted the philosophy of assisting developing countries but have been unable to give full effect to what has been accepted intellectually.

Our external difficulties arise from tariffs, quota restrictions and other obstacles which prevent the expansion of our export trade.

The unfortunate fluctuations in prices of raw materials, with prices of manufactured goods showing steep and continual rise, aggravate the problem of our terms of trade.

The agricultural policies of developed countries allow for grant of substantial subsidies to assist their domestic products by way of protection, and to depress the international prices of agricultural commodities to the disadvantage of developing countries.

Also, the developed countries have shown reluctance to vacate the field of simple manufactures, with the unfortunate result that the unsophisticated manufactured goods of developing countries are left with inadequate external markets.

Such industry as we have been able to set up with loans obtained from developed countries is unable to generate foreign exchange earnings sufficiently to enable us to meet our growing foreign debt obligations.

Recently published statistics show that in 32 less developed countries the debt liability now absorbs seven per cent of the export earnings as compared with only three per cent in 1955.

There is no doubt now that external aid programs, though admittedly of great assistance to developing economies, are inadequate for balanced economic growth and will have to be supplemented.

To provide aid and to deny trade to less developed countries amounts almost to giving with one hand what is taken away with the other.

Therefore, if we are to solve the balance of payments problems of the less developed world, we must explore possibilities of adopting new trade patterns and of according preference in markets of advanced countries to manufactures of developing countries.

A recent United Nations survey indicates that if developed countries were to purchase $10 billion worth of manufactures by 1980 from under-developed countries, this would substantially benefit the latter, although the transaction would represent just one per cent of the additional demand for manufacturers in the world.

The creation of export opportunities in developed countries for under-developed countries should not require extraordinary effort or sacrifice on the part of the former.

We should, therefore, consider the linking up of questions of aid and trade, as neither by itself would be enough, and both would need to be harnessed to achieve the goals we all have in mind.

These are some of our common internal and external problems. What is going to be our approach to them is a searching question which we must ask ourselves in all earnestness. The situation will demand concerted and sustained effort on our part over a long period.

Internally, we must reform our educational and social systems, our outmoded ways of agriculture, our administrative machinery and our way of life generally. And we must mobilize all the resources available to us for an all-out attack on the appalling poverty, ignorance and disease with which we are faced today.

Externally, we should urge developed countries to accept structural changes in their economies so that sectors of simple manufactures are vacated in favor of developing countries to enable them to improve their export earnings, meet their increasing foreign debt obligations and enlarge their capacity for import of more sophisticated manufactures from developed countries.

We should also urge developed countries to make their contribution towards stabilization of prices of raw materials so that developing countries which produce them can establish long-term programs on reasonably safe assumptions and estimates of earnings.

New trade patterns and economic relations will need to be evolved. It should be clear to men of perception that lopsided economic development is not in the larger interests of the world, not even of those who gain thereby in the short run.

We are engaged in a gigantic struggle for economic emancipation which has no parallel in human history. Let us have no illusions about the sacrifice that the struggle will involve. Let us make the effort equal to the task ahead of us. History will judge us harshly if we fail to make the effort. Let history not judge us so.

Let us demonstrate, together where we can, alone where we must, that we are determined to make the sacrifices which the attainment of our goal demands of us.

ANATOMY OF DEVELOPMENT*

OUR people must help themselves by working for socio-economic development of the nation. The need for such development is a permanent challenge and without it no nation can be strong enough to defend it or sustain its freedom. Nor can it hold its ground in this fast moving world.

The problems of socio-economic development are so varied and so stupendous that no Government can tackle them alone. The nation as a whole must understand them and work for their solution unitedly.

We are a nation of some 100 million people. The overwhelming majority of our people, some 80 per cent, lives in rural areas and is dependent on agriculture for its living. Educationally, we have a great leeway to make, particularly in scientific and technical spheres. Industrially, we have made considerable progress, especially after 1958, but we have yet to build a broad industrial base. We are particularly deficient in heavy industries.

Our resources are limited and it is, therefore, extremely necessary to husband them meticulously and to put them to the best possible use. That is where the need for careful and intelligent planning comes in. We have had two Five-Year Plans[1]; the second is due to expire in 1965. We have recorded substantial gains, particularly in the course of the Second Plan. The rate of growth of national income has doubled. There are other accepted economic and social indices by which the progress of a country is judged. And by almost all the criteria, we have moved ahead. In consumption per head of the food-grains, cloth and other commodities, the rise is significant.

* From a broadcast, January 1964.
[1] The First Five Year Plan related to years 1955 to 1960, and the Second Five Year Plan to years 1960 to 1965.

We are using almost 500 per cent more iron and steel, and over 70 per cent more cement than in the past. The increase in transport is 50 per cent. These are indices of well-being, of progress, of rising prosperity.

Not only have national income and consumption increased, there has also been a steady rise in national investment. We have incurred vast expenditures on building the social overheads necessary for the development of the country. Water and land development programs have brought nearly two million acres of new land under cultivation, and have improved the water supply of many million acres of old land. The installed power generation has increased 400 per cent, and the new works in progress will add almost another half a million kilowatts to our power supply. Plans are in hand to make important additions to this supply, including nuclear generation.

The mileage of high grade roads, the number of rail cars and the telecommunication facilities have all multiplied rapidly.

The number of schools has increased by the thousand. New universities, including technical universities, have been opened and more are in the planning stage. Professional colleges, polytechniques and vocational schools are coming up as scheduled in the Second Plan. And in several sectors we hope to achieve the targets ahead of the Plan timings. The Plan target for food and agriculture has been exceeded three years ahead of the schedule.

TRADE VERSUS AID*

I T is a healthy sign that private enterprise in Pakistan is coming forward to assume greater responsibility for economic and research studies. The Government has placed heavy reliance on private enterprise in the execution of industrial development programs, and I have no doubt that the private sector will continue to play an appropriate role in the implementation of the Third Five Year Plan[1] also. The rate of growth can be sustained and improved upon only by maintaining a balance between private and public sectors consistent with the requirements of the economy. These requirements are dynamic; and this necessitates that the "balance" should be kept under constant watch. We cannot afford to adopt a dogmatic or doctrinaire approach. We must be pragmatic in demarcating the spheres of economic activity available to the two sectors and in defining their inter-relationship from time to time.

During the last few years, the Government has established a sound framework for national reconstruction with the full participation of the people. Significant advances have been made not only in social and political life but also in the economic sphere. The welfare of the common man has been the principal objective of all development policies.

The problem of promotion of trade between developed and developing countries is a matter of critical importance for all Afro-Asian countries which must secure expanding markets for their manufactures. The industrially developed countries have to concede a reasonable share of trade in manufactures to developing countries. Unless this is done, programs of aid and assistance will make little sense.

The stage has come when we should begin to substitute

---

* From the inaugural address, Economic Development Seminar, Lahore, March 1964.
[1] The Third Five Year Plan relates to years 1965 to 1970.

trade for aid to the mutual and long-term advantage of both the developed and developing countries. The dilemma of developing countries must be understood and resolved. It is distressing to find that the efforts of these countries to implement economic programs are being neutralized by restrictive attitudes of some developed countries. It is in the interests of world economy to allow the legitimate expectations of developing countries to materialize. I sincerely hope that developed countries will respond to this challenging situation and adopt outward looking trading policies to help developing countries meet their financial obligations and improve their balance of payments position.

The central point in this decade of development is this: if we mean well for three-fourths of the human race who live in Asia and Africa, then developing countries must be enabled to pay their own way in moving towards self-sustained economic growth.

Conscious of the limitations imposed on us within the existing pattern of world trade, we have been trying to find new markets wherever possible. All efforts are being made for the diversification of trade. It is now for the private sector to seize the opportunity to play its part in the promotion of our export earnings.

The Third Five-Year Plan envisages implementation of a sizeable program for establishment of new industries and also provides for operation of existing industries at full capacity. At the same time, allocations to the agriculture section are being increased considerably so that, with improved economic and social overheads, we should be able to generate additional incomes in the rural economy. Prosperity in the rural areas will be the acid test of our development plans and a necessary condition of future growth of the industrial sector.

The emerging nations of Asia and Africa should remember that, in the ultimate analysis, self-help and mutual help alone would effectively and unfailingly lead their countries to balanced economic growth.

ECONOMIC BREAK-THROUGH*

THE reviews of the working of the Second Five Year Plan, which the Government has recently carried out, indicate that the Plan targets have either been reached or are within sight of attainment. The current year is likely to show an over six per cent increase in gross national product which is the highest we have ever attained in any single year. We believe we are also witnessing a break-through in agriculture. We have moved forward in industry and there has been significant improvement in our foreign exchange reserves. At long last, divine benevolence and our endeavors are beginning to show results.

The economy today presents a healthy and cheerful contrast to the nearly bankrupt economy of five years ago. In the last three years, national income has risen at a rate which is nearly double the rate of population growth. During the current year national income is expected to increase by about seven per cent, which is perhaps the highest rate of growth attained by any developing country at any time. Some improvement is already visible in the way our people are living today: in food, clothing, housing, education, transport and other amenities of life that they enjoy. This is an improvement that will be cumulative: its impact is slow at first but increases rapidly and encompasses the entire community as development proceeds, imparting to the country a new outlook towards life and a new sense of national dignity, and preparing it for further endeavors to achieve higher national goals.

What is most gratifying is that we are achieving a satisfactory rate of growth with much greater reliance on our own efforts than was ever thought possible. We shall not only be fulfilling our pledge to raise the required domestic resources for the Second Plan; we shall be raising more and shall also

* From a broadcast, May 1964.

be spending more from our own foreign exchange reserves
on development.

This is a tribute to those who have saved and reinvested
their incomes and also to millions of those who quietly paid
the rising taxes so that the national effort may expand and
may command international support and commendation.

Our exports are likely to exceed the Plan target. Exports
have been increasing at an annual rate of about seven per cent
as against two per cent forecast in the Plan, so that we, as a
nation, have moved increasingly towards a position of via-
bility. Currently, we are financing over 30 per cent of our
development imports from our own foreign exchange resources, and I am sure that this percentage will increase
steadily and we will be able to relieve our friends proportion-
ately of the need to finance our development effort.

It is no small measure of the confidence that the outside
world has in Pakistan's destiny that it has pledged more than
$2 billion of economic assistance to Pakistan in one form or
another during the first four years of the Second Plan. I am
glad that we are living up to this confidence.

My Government has consistently accorded full political
support to socio-economic planning and made socio-economic
development the primary goal of all its efforts. I think that
we can take legitimate pride in the prospect not only of
implementing the Second Plan but also of over-fulfilling some
of its targets. And I feel that the nation must pay a tribute
to those thousands of silent workers—whether engaged in
the formation of plans or in their execution—who have
gone about their task with a rare sense of dedication and who
have worked tirelessly for the betterment of our country.

PEACE THROUGH PROSPERITY*

I N our quest for world peace we sometimes forget that economic well-being is a necessary pre-condition. If peace is
to be brought to the world, poverty must be banished from
all corners of the globe. As peace has today become indivisible,
so have prosperity of the rich nations and economic well-being
of developing nations become interdependent.

Recently, a World Bank report on Pakistan identified it as
being among the outstanding examples of a dynamic, developing economy. This is a flattering observation. We have reached
this point after years of disappointment. Consider the time
when we started our independent existence in 1947. The world
then looked askance at what it thought was an impudent
adventure to establish a new state, without much prospect of
a viable economy, by a people inexperienced in administration,
unacquainted with modern technology, and lacking both the
capital and natural resources for development. But our people
did not share these misgivings. They had faith in their future
and, in spite of the misfortunes and setbacks of the last 17
years, they can today look with a degree of satisfaction upon
what they have achieved.

Pakistan's economy is largely agricultural. Besides food
crops we grow jute, tea and cotton. Our major industrial
resource is natural gas, of which we possess considerable
quantities.

I shall divide this survey of Pakistan's development into two
periods. The first period ranges from our independence in
1947 to 1958. During this period our main effort was directed
towards building up the infrastructure for development. We
created a number of consumer industries, the most important
of which was textiles. The First Five-Year Plan for develop-

* From an address at Overseas Development Institute, London, July 1964.

ment was launched in 1955, and the economy registered a growth rate of 2.2 per cent per annum up to 1958. This growth rate, however, just about matched the population increase, leaving the country unfortunately no more prosperous than it was formerly.

The first task which my Government addressed itself to in 1958 was to increase agricultural production. The very first measure undertaken was the rationalization of land holdings. Pakistan had inherited a land tenure system which, on the one hand, allowed fragmentation of land holdings to an uneconomic size and, on the other, placed no ceiling on the maximum acreage a person could own. We set not only a maximum ceiling on holdings to discourage feudalistic control and absentee landlordism but also, much more important, we fixed a minimum size for holdings of agricultural land. Economically, this was necessary; it also ensured social justice. Concurrently, the program for the use of fertilizers was intensified by paying subsidies as high as 50 per cent of the cost to farmers. Our efforts have been rewarded with a gratifying increase in agricultural production from 1958 onwards; the index today stands at 139 against 107 in 1958.

The chief problems of agriculture in West Pakistan are two-fold. First, the shortage of irrigation water. This shortage was further accentuated when in a recent settlement with India we lost the use of waters of two of our five rivers. To replace this loss we are currently engaged in the construction of link canals and new storage capacity on the Jhelum and the Indus rivers. This has necessitated the undertaking of a tremendous works program ranging over 10 years at a cost of $1.8 billion—the largest hydrological works program in the world today.

The second problem is that of continuous salination of agricultural lands. Salinity and water-logging make their appearance sooner or later in irrigated areas on account of seepage of water from the canals. West Pakistan is losing one acre of cultivated land through water-logging and salinity every five minutes. We have already lost land area of about 4.7 million acres out of a total cultivable area of 25 million acres.

To combat this menace, some three years ago we welcomed a highpowered scientific and technical team from the United States Government. This team has made an ambitious set of recommendations. One anti-salinity project has already been launched in an area covering 13 million acres of land. It was found that an area of at least this size would have to be treated initially to make an immediate impact on the water table as well as on salinity.

In East Pakistan, apart from floods which come down the rivers, and these are mighty rivers, something like nine million acres are under water in a land mass of 54,000 square miles. Much silt comes down the rivers and the beds have risen by nine feet in some places. It is amazing what havoc water can do in a limited space. Also, in East Pakistan there is frequent flooding from sea water, and we have constructed something like 1,100 miles of coastal embankments to make the land safe from seepage and from infiltration of sea water.

Since 1958, Pakistan has developed maturity not only in consumer industries set up during the First Five-Year Plan, but also in productive industries, such as petro-chemicals, pharmaceuticals, fertilizers, ship building, petroleum refining, and the like. We are beginning to think seriously in terms of a heavy industrial complex, steel and electronics. Power generation in Pakistan has risen four-fold since 1958. The industrial sector now contributes about 15 per cent to national income; its annual rate of growth varies from 10 to 12 per cent. This change from an agricultural to an industrial economy imparts a firmness to the economy as it obviates—at least partly—the effects of fluctuations in agricultural production due to weather and natural calamities. Agricultural output is improving, and current prospects are that the economy can look forward to a growth rate of at least five per cent in a year of normal crops and a much higher rate in years of favorable weather conditions. Gross national product increased at the rate of 4.3 per cent during 1960 to 1963. Last year it registered an increase of six to seven per cent. At the rate at which we are progressing we shall double the national output in 16 years. Our sights are, however, set much higher and in our Perspective Plan, which has been drawn up for the period 1965 to 1985, the goal is to triple the national income. Only thus can we hope to provide a minimum standard of decent living to our people within one generation.

The present pattern of world trade poses for Pakistan, in common with the other developing countries, a serious problem. The prices of our agricultural raw materials have declined over the years while the prices of manufactures which we import from developed countries have been rising steadily. According to one calculation, Pakistan in this process suffered a loss of about $1.3 billion in the 1950-60 decade while in the same period the quantum of foreign aid of all kinds, including technical assistance, amounted almost to $1.3 billion. In addition, we received $457 million in loans and credits which are to be repaid. In other words, more than three-quarters of the aid received was offset by losses in terms of trade.

Concurrently with the problem of commodity prices, there is the other equally grave problem of disposal of our industrial products in international markets. If we are to finance from our own resources our future growth, it is imperative that we should increase our exports at the rate of at least six to seven per cent per annum in the coming years. Since the demand for agricultural raw materials is inelastic and prices uncertain, we have to make a major effort to find markets for our manufactures and semi-manufactures. Our efforts in this direction can succeed only if industrially advanced countries adopt outward looking policies and not impose tariffs, quota restrictions, internal taxes or other artificial barriers on our exports.

At the last Commonwealth Prime Ministers meeting[1] I ventured to pose a question to the international community, and in particular to Western industrialized nations: were they prepared to change the existing unsatisfactory pattern of international trade which was, in effect, tantamount to economic imperialism of the worst kind?

I warned the Western world that the consequences of the short-sighted policy of denying our manufactures access to their markets would be disastrous.

I must confess that I am disappointed that industrialized nations on the whole have failed to meet the challenge of the times, which is to ensure the minimum economic development of two-thirds of the world. One hopeful outcome of the UN conference on trade and development held recently in Geneva has been that a number of industrialized countries have demonstrated their goodwill by accepting the fundamentals of the requirements, and a forum has been created where, let us hope, the problem can be dealt with in a more meaningful manner.

It seems to me that having accepted that the international community owes it to itself and to the peace and prosperity of the world to come to the assistance of developing countries, the implications that follow from the acceptance of this basic philosophy have either not been realized or have been accepted with mental reservations. Take the question of financial assistance. It is not only the quantum of assistance but also the terms on which such assistance is provided that is of fundamental importance. And yet today we see the spectacle of tied loans and of loans which are little more than suppliers' credit and whose main purpose is to promote the exports of industrialized countries under the umbrella of aid. I am not denying that even this form of assistance has played a useful role. But let us not forget the strain this places on the economies of developing countries. Let us not forget the burden

[1] September 1962.

which is added to debt servicing problems and the increase in prices which is inherent in tied aid. In this connection, I am amazed to find that just when the majority of poorer countries have started their development programs, the capital-exporting countries are displaying signs of tiredness. Nothing is more calculated to undo the benefits which have accrued than doubts and difficulties about terms and continuity in aid programs.

To the best of our ability we are trying to keep the covenant with our people to provide for them the basic needs for a decent human existence. Our friends, too, have helped us to meet this challenge. We are sincerely grateful for what they have done for us, and are resolved and determined to do the rest ourselves.

I have repeatedly quoted to my people a verse from the Holy Quran. I would like to repeat it here again:

The Lord changeth not what is with a people until the people change what is in themselves.

ECONOMIC LIBERALISM*

ONE of the distinguishing features of our age is the fierce struggle going on everywhere for the conquest of man's mind. This struggle extends not only to the ideological field but also beyond to the social and economic spheres of life. It is a grim struggle, and in the economic field the outcome will determine the means which the developing nations adopt to achieve rapid progress. Will they adopt a liberal philosophy or will they be driven to authoritarian controls? The West has no choice but to join this struggle and strive to demonstrate that economic growth can be combined with individual freedom. It is in this context that the relationship between developed Western countries and developing nations of Asia and Africa today assumes a new significance.

Foreign assistance is more than a humanitarian gesture. It is a powerful weapon in Western strategy to ensure that economic growth in newly developing countries proceeds within the framework of liberal economic and social institutions. Pakistan today is one of the most successful examples of a developing country achieving rapid progress with the help of foreign assistance. During our Second Plan the Western world has provided over £700 million ($1,960 million) of economic aid. This has enabled us to achieve high rates of growth without being driven to desperate measures. It has meant a tremendous national effort but at least it was not unbearable.

In the last five years the country has saved and reinvested over one-fifth of the additional incomes generated by economic growth. In a country as poor as ours there is always tremendous pressure to increase consumption as incomes increase. But we had to resist this pressure for the sake of economic growth. To do so we have had to levy additional taxes amounting to nearly £140 million ($392 million) in

* First appeared in The London Times Review of Industry, September 1964.

the last five years and to increase our exports at the rate of
six per cent a year. It is by no means an easy task to tax an
economy enjoying a per capita income of only £25 ($70)
a year, or to divert an increasing proportion of domestic
production to the export market. But many difficult political choices have to be made in the interest of economic
development.

The growth rate in national income over the last four years
has been above five per cent a year, which is about twice as
high as the present rate of increase in population. This holds
out the promise of improving average living standards to a
fairly respectable level in the next decade or so. These growth
rates are currently financed to the extent of 60 per cent by
domestic resources and 40 per cent by foreign assistance.
Of course we would have tried to mount a similar development effort even without foreign assistance, but the struggle
would have been harder and the economic institutions might
have had a different orientation. We have achieved these
growth rates within the framework of a liberal economic
philosophy. In fact, our approach to economic planning has
been pragmatic all along. It has been the constant endeavor
of the Government to mobilize the creative energies of the
nation and to give all possible incentives for the stimulation
of private initiative. The Government has limited its own role
to providing a suitable framework for the private sector and
to the creation of those facilities which the private sector
has neither the ability nor the willingness to develop.

There have been no grand experiments in nationalization,
no fancy slogans about socialism, no undue intervention in
the private sector. In fact, the Government has gradually
removed most of the administrative and bureaucratic controls
which hampered progress of the private sector. Over 90 per
cent of total national production is actually in private hands.
We have encouraged private initiative not only because we
are committed to a liberal philosophy of life but because

the private sector has delivered the goods. In a poor economy like ours people do not generally indulge in the luxury of asking ideological questions. They are far too preoccupied in the desperate struggle for survival. What matters to them is the visible impact of economic development on their daily lives, not theologies of capitalism or socialism. Only if the new class of entrepreneur, grown rapidly rich, refrains from conspicuous consumption and ostentatious living and reinvests the profits in expansion and new enterprises will it be acceptable to society; the pursuit of private profits must proceed within the framework of national interests. Fortunately, this has been generally the case in Pakistan.

The faith of the Western world in Pakistan's economic progress is evident from the generous assistance provided for our development plans, particularly in the last five years. But deeply as we appreciate this, we are still hoping for a whole new concept of foreign assistance geared more closely to the needs of developing economies. Many of the loans provided to us still carry terms which are hard. These loans are generally tied to the donor countries which considerably raise their cost. We are hopeful that the attitudes in the Western world will change. Despite the disappointing outcome of the recent Geneva conference on trade and development, we hope that interest rates can gradually be lowered and repayment periods prolonged.

We also hope that the world will get away from the current practice of "tying" the source of procurement so that international trade can be free and no artificial barriers are raised in the way of a genuinely multilateral system of payments. But foreign assistance alone is not the answer. The grand alliance between developed and developing countries has to extend far beyond into the sphere of foreign trade. We are just as keen as our friends abroad to bring our dependence on foreign assistance to a speedy end, but this much desired consummation can be achieved only if we are enabled to enter freely the markets of the Western world. A world where quota restrictions and tariff walls are raised against the products of poorer economies will not only be an inhuman world; it will also be a strangely unreal one as it would become increasingly difficult for the credit importing countries to meet their debt obligations. In fact the lending countries must accept the repayment of tied loans in the form of exports.

For instance, Pakistan's long-term plan to triple national income over the next 20 years calls for a four-fold increase in exports. A large part of these exports will be manufactured goods, since the scope for raw material exports is fairly limited. It is only if the protectionist tendencies do not gain ground in the Western world and tariff walls do not go up all around that we can hope to reach our goals. Of course there is always the possibility for developing countries to increase trade between themselves. We shall certainly take full advantage of this. It is too early, perhaps, to think of close-knit institutional economic arrangements covering the entire Afro-Asian region but this is the grand conception that often dominates our thoughts. It is within this large context that we have made a modest beginning recently by proposing concrete arrangements for regional economic cooperation between Turkey, Iran and Pakistan. It is our earnest hope that the area of this cooperative effort increases and extends to many other countries.

While we are highly appreciative of the assistance we have received for development so far, we are committed to reduce the element of foreign financing in our future plans so that over the next 20 years we carry on development primarily from our own resources. The Western world can help us in this endeavor by evolving a more enlightened concept of foreign assistance and foreign trade. This will ensure that economic growth continues to proceed within a liberal framework and the developing countries, urged on by their desperate needs, are not driven to rash experiments.

REGIONAL COOPERATION *

THE idea embodied in the Istanbul agreement signed by Turkey, Iran and Pakistan is by no means a new concept.[1] I do not claim its authorship either. But our assessment has always been that the future of smaller countries in Asia is bleak indeed unless they get together and form cohesive associations in order to be in a position to resist the pressure of the major powers in Asia. Look at the picture of Asia today. What do you see? Mighty countries are emerging—Russia, China and India. India with something like 500 million people, China with over 700 million people, and Russia a very powerful country indeed. On the other side you see many smaller countries of Asia, poor in resources, struggling to overcome their manifold disabilities.

Now, if any of the three major Asian powers decided to expand, where will they expand? Can they expand into the empty spaces of South America or Australia? They can't. They can't because those areas are strong enough to defend themselves. They can only expand—it is only logical—at the cost of the smaller countries, either for the sake of power or for the sake of acquisition of material and natural wealth.

The smaller countries in Asia will always remain vulnerable and will always be under pressure, just as we in Pakistan have been living for the last 17 years under the shadow of Indian aggression and oppression. That will be the history of all smaller Asian countries, unless wisdom prevails and these countries get together to present a bigger base and a bigger unity. If pressures then develop against these countries, they should be able to resist effectively.

* From a speech, Lahore, October 1964.
[1] On July 20, 1964, an agreement was signed at Istanbul between Turkey, Iran and Pakistan establishing special machinery for cooperative action, known as the Regional Cooperation for Development.

If you agree with this analysis, then one is entitled to ask: what is the future of the countries in the Middle East, and especially, what is the future of Turkey, Iran, Afghanistan and Pakistan? It would be a wonderful thing if all countries in the Middle East appreciated the need for a common under- standing. But if they don't, at least these four countries should make an endeavor to find a unity of purpose. And that has been my dream for a long time.

When Pakistan joined the Baghdad Pact[2] I had a good deal to do with it, a good deal to do with friendship with Turkey, friendship with Iran, and friendship with Iraq; and I felt that here was an opportunity for the Muslims of the world and of these regions to come together on one platform. It was the first time in the history of the two major religions— Christianity and Islam—that the Christian world was looking for the support of the Muslim world for its own safety.

We joined the Baghdad Pact, and I thought at the time that if the Arab world were also to join us, a great service would be done to Islam. But some of the Arab leaders spoke of the Pact as a trap. How could the Pact have harmed them? There never was any intention to harm the Arabs. Certainly there was no such intention on the part of Pakistan. We genuinely felt that here was the right course to take and that, if it was taken, a great deal of good would follow.

Well, the turn of events brought Iran, Turkey and Pakistan together in a new combination. We gained much from this association. We came to know each other at different levels and that generated mutual confidence and goodwill.

The Istanbul agreement is also a child of events, born of mutual trust through long association in varied spheres.

Let me explain to you the philosophy of getting together as I see it. What is the right way of getting together? The right way is that you should get together in non-political and non-controversial fields. Once you have political tie-ups, bick-

2 July 1955.

ering starts; and you make one compromise after another till the common denominator becomes the common weakness of all. Therefore, I am extremely mindful that we do not have an arrangement whereby we inherit each other's weaknesses. If ever a closer association develops between these three or four countries in the future, and if I have anything to do with it, I shall do it on the principle that I have just enumerated. But if I am not there, then I think you must know that the way it should be done must be not to allow common weaknesses to become the running pattern of these countries. And I believe that the best way would be this. Define the spheres in which you wish to collaborate. Having defined them, create an executive authority headed by the Head of State of each country in rotation—three or four years' term. Do not have a common legislature. Whenever major decisions are taken by the executive body, secure their ratification from the respective legislatures of the countries.

In establishing an organization for the implementation of the agreement on Regional Cooperation for Development (RCD), I took care to ensure that it should not be top heavy. It should, I felt, be simple and manageable so that the region's interests are effectively and expeditiously promoted. We earmarked 10 different spheres, where collaboration is possible between Turkey, Iran and Pakistan. I think, so far, the results have been very encouraging indeed.

I am sure you will wish this venture success as I do. Voluntary and close collaboration between Muslim nations has been the dream of some of the greatest Muslims in the world and, if this venture succeeds, the dream will be coming true.

Index

Abdullah, Sheikh, 48, 60

Afghanistan, 14, 15, 76, 104

Africa, 37, 40, 58, 60, 90, 99

Afro-Asian Economic Conference, 83n

Agreement of Cooperation, 17, 18

Ali, Mohammad, 19

All-India Muslim League, 3, 7

Assam, 25, 26, 47, 49, 61, 73, 74

Australia, 17, 103

Baghdad Pact, 17, 20, 104

Basic democracies, xi, 9-10

Birch Grove, 25, 34n

Burma, 76

Calcutta, see West Bengal

Central Treaty Organization (CENTO), 17, 20

Ceylon, 24, 76

China, 17
  and India, 22-8 passim, 37, 38, 47, 71, 72
  and Pakistan, 76
  and United States, 37, 38

Colombo proposals, 73

Colonialism, xii, 13-14, 40

Commonwealth Prime Ministers meeting, 97

Communication, 7, 83, 88

Communism, 13, 37-8

Congress party, 78

Constitution Commission of Pakistan, The, 10-11

Constitution of 1956, 7, 11

East Pakistan, xi, 5, 17, 29, 30, 49, 56, 95

East Pakistan Rifles, 49

Economic Development Seminar, 89n

Economic growth, 94, 96, 99, 100, 101
  advances, 89, 90, 91
  problems, 4, 83-4

Education, 13, 88

Five Year Plan, First (1955-1960), 87, 93-4, 95

Five Year Plan, Second (1960-1965), 87, 88, 91, 92, 99, 101

Five Year Plan, Third (1965-1970), xii, 13, 89, 90

Foreign Affairs, 3n, 17n

France, 17

Geneva, 97, 101

Goa, 32, 33

Great Britain, 14, 17
aid to India, 24, 25, 26, 27, 72
and Sino-Indian dispute, 71

Hazratbal shrine, 47

Hindus, 18, 30, 49, 55, 61, 66

Holy Quran, 52, 98

Hyderabad, 32

India
agression of, 30, 31, 32, 33, 76, 103
conflict with China, 23-8, 30, 37, 71-6 *passim*
and Great Britain, 24, 25, 32, 72
and Kashmir, 29, 30, 31, 51, 71 *see also* India, relations with Pakistan
military aid, 23-8 *passim*, 32-4, 72-3, 75, 78
military build-up in, 34, 39, 47, 73, 74
military expenses, 51, 65, 67, 74, 75, 77, 78
relations with Pakistan, 14, 15, 16, 29, 33, 39, 62, 63, 64-5
and security of Pakistan, 18, 23, 28, 29, 30, 32-3, 47, 74, 76, 77
and Soviet Union, 20, 21, 73
sphere of influence, 19, 22, 29
and United States, 21, 22, 23, 25, 72 *see also* India, military aid

Indian press, 24n, 28n, 54, 60, 73-4

Indus river, 94

Iqbal. Dr. Muhammad, 3, 4

Iran, 17, 102, 103, 104, 105

Iraq, 17, 104

Islam, ix, 3-4, 8, 11, 52, 98, 104, 105

Istanbul agreement, *see* Regional Cooperation for Development

Jammu, *see* Kashmir

Jhelum river, 94

Jinnah, Quaid-i-Azam Mahomed Ali, 3, 6, 7, 32

Junagadh, 31

Karachi, 83n

Kashmir, xii
Action Committee, 58
change of government in, 54, 59
and Indo-Pakistan relations, 15, 29, 30, 33-4, 51, 54, 64-5, 71, 75-6
instrument of "accession", 31
joint communique on, 19, 20
military cost to India, 51, 54, 67
plebescite in, 19, 20, 31, 48-9, 55-6, 59
and Security Council, 20, 21, 29, 34, 48, 51, 52, 55, 56, 58, 61, 77
self determination, 5, 51-5, 58-61, 76
and United Nations, 20, 52, 56-57, 58

Khan, Liaquat Ali, 6

Ladakh, 24, 25

Lahore, 40n, 89n, 103n

Land reform, x, 13, 94

Laos, 37

London, 37n, 93n

London Times Review of Industry, The, 99n

MacMahon Line, 25

Martial Law, 11, 12

Mohammad, Bakhshi Ghulam, 48

Muslims, Indian, 3, 6, 30, 47, 49, 50, 61, 65, 66, 74

Mutual Defense Assistance Agreement, 17, 20, 23

Nanpuria, N. J., 28n

Nassau, 25

National income, 87, 88, 91, 95, 96, 100, 102 *see also* Per capita income

Nationalism, xii, 6, 40

Nehru, Jawaharlal, 18, 19, 20, 24, 27, 30, 31, 32, 34n, 63

Nepal, 76

New Zealand, 17

North Atlantic Treaty Organization (NATO), 33

Northeast Frontier Agency (NEFA), 24, 25, 26

North Vietnam, 38

North West Frontier Province, former, 56

Overseas Development Institute, 93n

Per capita income, 83, 100 *see also* National income

Philippines, 17

Population, 3, 5, 87
growth of, 13, 83, 94, 100

Portugal, 32

Potter, Philip, 27n

Presidential Manifesto, ixn

Private sector, 89, 90, 100, 101

Radcliffe, Cyril, 5

Rawalpindi, 71n

Reddy, Sanjiva, 29n

Regional Cooperation for Development (RCD), 103n, 104, 105

Republic of Congo, 56

Security Council, 20, 21, 29, 32n, 34, 48, 51, 52, 55, 56, 58, 61, 77

Shamsuddin government, 54

Shastri, Lal Bahadur, 78

South East Asia Treaty Organization (SEATO), 17

South Vietnam, 37, 38

Soviet Union, 17, 27
aid to India, 24, 26, 73
and Kashmir, 20, 21
relations with Pakistan, 76
and Sino-Indian dispute, 74, 75

Stevenson, Adlai, 32n

Tauhid (Unity of God), 4

Thailand, 17

Thana Council, 9

Times of India, 24n, 34n

Tibet, 38-9

Trade policies, 84, 85, 86, 89, 90, 96, 97, 101, 102

Tripura, 47, 49, 61, 74

Turkey, 17, 102, 103, 104, 105

Union Council and Town Committee, 9, 10

Union of Soviet Socialist Republics (USSR), *see* Soviet Union

United Kingdom (UK), *see* Great Britian

United Nations, 20, 21, 33, 43, 52, 56, 57, 58, 85 *see also* Security Council

United Nations Commission for India and Pakistan (UNCIP), xii, 56

United Nations Conference on Trade and Development, 97, 101

United States
  aid to India, 21, 23-8, 72
  alliances with Pakistan, 17-20
  change in foreign policy, 21-3
  image in Asia, 22, 79
  and Sino-Indian clashes, 71, 74
  technical aid to Pakistan, 95

Viceregal Lodge, 5

West Bengal, 49, 61

West Pakistan, xi, xii, 5, 12, 17, 30, 94-5

White Paper, *Kashmir and the United Nations*, 29-30

World Bank report, 93

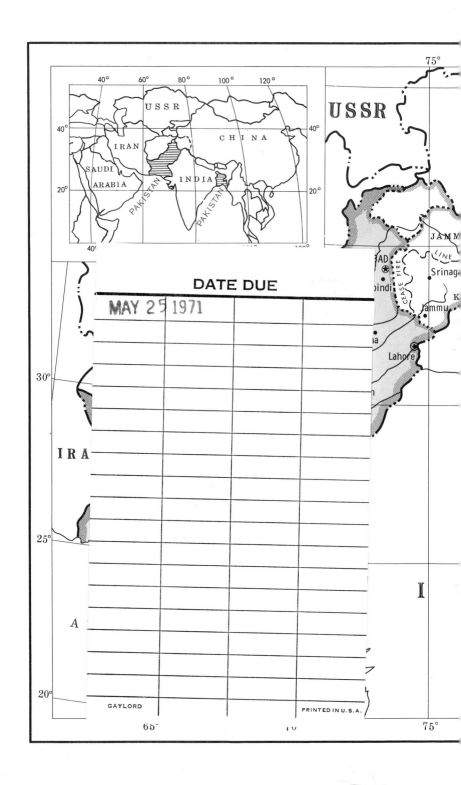

USSR

40° 60° 80° 100° 120°

USSR

IRAN

CHINA

SAUDI
ARABIA

PAKISTAN

INDIA

PAKISTAN

40°

20°

JAMM

LINE

Srinag

CEASE FIRE

K

AD

pindi

Jammu

DATE DUE

MAY 25 1971

a

Lahore

30°

IRA

25°

I

A

20°

GAYLORD

PRINTED IN U.S.A.

65°

75°

75°